Foreword

All business organisations must understand the importance of facilities management if they are to ensure that the operation of their estates is cost effective, delivers value for money and supports the strategic aims of their businesses. This is particularly true of further education colleges which operate from a diverse range of premises and which are often trying to reconcile the conflicting aims of improving the quality and range of educational provision while seeking to increase cost efficiency and improve value for money in the utilisation and operation of their estates.

The publication of *Effective Facilities Management: A Good Practice Guide* will help colleges achieve better value for money by helping them to understand the importance of facilities management and in the adoption of up-to-date and modern techniques in its implementation. It will also help them to assess and identify potential efficiency gains and the transfer of risks in the operation and management of the services they require.

This guide should also demonstrate to the providers of facilities management services, whether as a consultant or contractor, that the further education sector is determined to ensure that effective facilities management is recognised as an important priority by colleges.

Paul Orchard-Lisle MA, TD, FRICS

President of the Council of the University of Reading
Past president of the Royal Institution of Chartered Surveyors
Senior Partner, Healey and Baker

Good Practice Guides

The FEFC and the NAO have commissioned a series of good practice guides which offer guidance and practical advice for further education colleges and others on various aspects of college management. The publications currently available in this series are:

Estate Management in Further Education Colleges: A Good Practice Guide (HMSO 1996; price £13.95)

Procurement: A Good Practice Guide (TSO 1997; price £15.95)

A further title, *Marketing: A Good Practice Guide* is forthcoming.

Effective Facilities Management

A Good Practice Guide

London: The Stationery Office

Prepared by the University of Reading in association with FBA Limited

**THE
FURTHER
EDUCATION
FUNDING
COUNCIL**

NAO
NATIONAL AUDIT OFFICE

Contents

HM Treasury has recommended the following guidelines to public sector organisations to ensure regularity and propriety in the handling of public funds.

- Don't bend or break the rules

- Put in place and follow clear procedures

- If approval is needed, get it first

- Don't allow a conflict of interests to affect, or appear to affect, decisions

- Don't use public money for private benefit

- Be even-handed

- Record the reasons for decisions

Introduction

Purpose and Background

Managing supporting services enables a college to function at its most efficient and effective level. Implicit in this management role are the issues of customer satisfaction and value for money. Facilities management is the focus for these issues and the impetus which led to the preparation of this guide.

In 1996, the Further Education Funding Council (the Council), in collaboration with the National Audit Office (NAO), commissioned a value-for-money study on contracting out estate-related services and facilities management. The study was essentially in two parts. The first was an examination of the value for money achieved by colleges in the provision of estate-related services and facilities management. The report, *Assessment of Value for Money Achieved by Colleges*, which was approved by the Council, highlights many issues and concerns. This guide — the second part of the study — shows how colleges can improve value for money whilst delivering customer satisfaction.

The Guide

The guide is a progressive look at how facilities management applies to colleges of all kinds. Other Council publications contain related guidance. This guide is not, therefore, intended to replace anything that has gone before; rather it is complementary. Within the guide are many examples of how facilities can be better managed, much of which is derived from practices known to work well elsewhere. Important in this respect is the need for individual colleges to consider the appropriateness of specific guidance where the size of an organisation would be a significant factor in either adopting or choosing not to adopt a particular course of action.

Acknowledgement

During the course of the study, the authors visited a cross-section of colleges to see how the various management teams were coping with their responsibilities. The knowledge gained has been used in preparing this guide. For this help and support, the authors would like to express their sincere appreciation.

Brian Atkin, The University of Reading
Adrian Brooks, FBA Limited
Reading, July 1997

What Is Facilities Management?

Introduction

1.1 Chapter 1 discusses the importance of facilities to an organisation and shows how facilities management can differ between colleges within the same sector. It also covers the requirement to secure value for money in the provision of services and outlines the attendant risks.

Policy Considerations

1.2 The following key issues need to be taken into consideration.

- the proper application of facilities management techniques will enable colleges to provide an appropriate environment for learning, teaching and training on a cost-effective and value-for money basis

- there are many definitions of facilities management. The one which best fits this guide is 'an integrated approach to operating, maintaining, improving and adapting the buildings and infrastructure of an organisation in order to create an environment that strongly supports the primary objectives of that organisation'

- if buildings and other facilities are not managed, this can begin to impact adversely upon the performance of colleges. Conversely, buildings and facilities have the potential to contribute towards providing the best environment for learning, teaching and training

- in practice, facilities management can cover a wide range of services, including property management, financial management, change management, human resources management, health and safety and contract management, in addition to building maintenance, domestic services (such as cleaning and security) and utilities supplies

- there is no universal approach to managing facilities. Each college — even within the same sector — will have different needs. Understanding those needs is key to effective facilities management, measured in terms of providing value for money

- quality of service or performance is a critical factor in any definition of value and, in this respect, the relationship between it and cost or price has to be better understood

- cost savings cannot be looked at in isolation. Colleges must be able to demonstrate what they are getting for their money, which is why value needs to be the focus of attention, not just cost

- risks to achieving value for money are many and should be transferred to those who are best able to manage them. This means that colleges should examine all options carefully and adopt those which are most likely to achieve the best value for money.

Guidance

Rationale for Facilities Management

1.3 Most buildings represent substantial investments for colleges and have to accommodate and support a range of activities, often taking into account competing needs. Within those activities is the core of the business of the college, that is, the creation of an environment to support learning, teaching and training in buildings which may not have been designed for the purposes for which they are now used. Yet, no matter how well focused a college might be on its core business, it cannot lose sight of the supporting services — the so-called non-core business.

1.4 Colleges may have already considered the distinction between their core and non-core businesses (such as cleaning and security) as part of the drive to deliver customer satisfaction and achieve better value for money. Since running a college, excluding academic staff costs, accounts for a significant part of the remaining annual expenditure, there is bound to be pressure to look for savings in non-core business areas. Cutting operating budgets may be a financial expedient, but this may not foster the long-term development of the college. Since the running of a college involves complex, co-ordinated processes and activities, the response has to be one of taking an integrated view. A piecemeal approach to cutting costs is unlikely to produce those savings and may impair the college's ability to deliver high-quality services.

1.5 In the past, it may have been possible for colleges to operate their buildings without giving them much management attention. Cleaning, maintenance, repairs and general caretaking duties were typical of the services which formed part of the day-to-day running of a college. Costs were met from various budgets, with concerns about them usually passed directly to the local education authority to act as it saw fit. Some colleges did, however, have delegated powers with respect to services, though this was by no means the general rule. The whole approach was largely one of reacting to events. Incorporation and new legislation have changed all of that. There has now been a fundamental shift in thinking from one of reaction to action.

1.6 Facilities management in further education can therefore be summarised as the creation of an environment that is conducive to learning, teaching and training, taking an integrated view of the services' infrastructure, and using this to deliver customer satisfaction and value for money through support for and enhancement of the core business. This definition can be developed to describe facilities management as something that will:

- sweat the assets, that is, make them highly cost effective

- provide competitive advantage to the core business of the college

- enhance the college culture and image

- enable future change in the use of space

- deliver effective and responsive services.

Defining Facilities Management

1.7   *Estate Management in Further Education Colleges: A Good Practice Guide* (FEFC/NAO 1996) adopts the definition produced by the British Institute of Facilities Management which defines facilities management as 'the practice of co-ordinating the physical workplace with the people and work of an organisation.' This simple and well-focused expression of facilities management does not, however, stress the contribution which well-managed facilities can make to an organisation. For the purpose of this guide, facilities management is 'an integrated approach to operating, maintaining, improving and adapting the buildings and infrastructure of an organisation in order to create an environment that strongly supports the primary objectives of that organisation' (adapted from Barrett (1995)). However, neither definition refers to the processes or activities which are associated with facilities management.

1.8   Facilities management has traditionally been seen as the poor relation of the property and construction professions. This is because it is understood in the old-fashioned sense of caretaking, cleaning, repairs and maintenance. In fact, it covers property management, financial management, change management, human resources management, health and safety and contract management, in addition to building and engineering services maintenance, domestic services and utilities supplies. These last three responsibilities are the most visible. The others are more subtle, though of no less importance. For facilities management to be effective, both the hard issues, for example financial regulation, and the soft issues, for example managing people, have to be considered.

Approaches to Facilities Management

1.9   From the study of the sample of further education colleges, through a detailed questionnaire and visits, ways in which colleges approach the management of their facilities have been identified. No two colleges approach facilities management in the same way. Although this conclusion is based on information from less than half of all colleges, the results can be considered representative of the sector. The study has also shown that colleges may not be aware of the extent to which value for money can be improved. This suggests that it is not the outcome which needs to be looked at closely, but the decision-making that leads to it.

1.10   There are common themes and approaches to facilities management, regardless of the size and location of buildings. However, a common approach may not necessarily result in common solutions to every problem. In some cases, estate-related services have been contracted out (outsourced) for good reason. In others, services are retained in house, again for good reason. There are, however, many colleges that operate what might be described as a mixed economy, which is where some services, even the same services, are contracted out in some measure as well as being retained in house.

1.11 Whichever course of action has been taken, the primary concern is the basis for the decision. Where the college's approach has been arrived at for entirely proper reasons, such as demonstrating better value for money from one approach as opposed to the other, facilities management is working effectively. It is how colleges reach their decision when choosing a particular approach that is of importance.

Informed or Intelligent Client Function

1.12 Colleges need to act as informed or intelligent clients if they are to be sure of delivering customer satisfaction and achieving best value for money. The informed or intelligent client function (ICF) is required irrespective of how facilities are procured. Annex A offers guidance on the role of the ICF.

Value for Money

1.13 The majority of colleges in the sample of those surveyed cite value for money as the determinant of whether or not to contract out a service or to retain it in house. Despite this, there is little evidence to suggest that colleges are aware of the extent to which they can improve value for money. Value is about the relationship between cost or price, and quality or performance. In many cases, however, value for money is simply equated with achieving a reduction in cost. Colleges may believe they are achieving value for money if they are paying less this year compared with the previous year.

1.14 Thus, value for money is often understood as being concerned with cost only. This is perhaps because cost is easier to measure. However, value for money is concerned with the economy, efficiency and effectiveness with which the services are delivered and the quality of those services. Colleges should, therefore, set themselves cost and quality objectives for the management of their facilities. In some cases, because of financial constraints, the cost objective will take priority over quality objectives.

1.15 When choosing options for service provisions and services providers, colleges need to include an assessment not only of cost implications, but quality (see paragraphs 5.29 to 5.31). Colleges should choose the approach and service providers offering best value, not simply lowest cost, and should measure performance against both cost and quality. Benchmarking can help in checking performance (see chapter 12).

1.16 Normally, the achievement of best value for money is demonstrated by acceptance of the lowest bid price in a competition where all other criteria (quality, performance, terms and conditions) are equal. Value for money can also be achieved through collaborative arrangements with suppliers and service providers. Bulk purchasing of utilities supplies — there can be economies of scale — is an obvious example and one that many colleges are pursuing. An additional benefit from collaboration is that risks are also shared.

1.17   Partnering is another kind of arrangement for procuring services where the opportunity exists to develop a strong relationship with a service provider which will ensure that best value for money is achieved whilst, at the same time, risks are better managed. Annex B outlines the case for partnering in the public sector, as contained in the government publication, *Setting New Standards* (HM Government 1995). Essentially, partnering is acceptable in terms of accountability if the following apply:

- there is competition at the outset in the choice of partners and periodic re-competition thereafter

- the partnering arrangement is established on the basis of clearly defined needs and objectives over a specified period

- there are specific and measurable milestones for improved performance as part of the contract, in order to demonstrate, through the use of benchmarking (see chapter 12), that value for money is being achieved.

1.18   There are options open to colleges beyond simply entering into price competitions each time a new supply or service is required or contract renewed. A college may, for instance, find that collaboration with other colleges improves negotiating and procurement powers. The particular merits of these arrangements and partnering are discussed in chapter 10.

Risk

1.19   In managing any organisation, there are many risks to meeting the business objectives; colleges are no exception. These risks have the potential to hinder, or even negate, attempts at achieving value for money.

1.20   Risks which colleges face include those shown in table 1 which includes references to the relevant chapters of this guide in which the underlying issues are considered. Some of these risks may be easier to address than others. In certain cases, colleges will need to acquire new skills or insights into how problems can be tackled.

Table 1. Risks faced by colleges in their facilities management

Risk	Chapter reference
Inadequately resourced or inexperienced client function	1, 2, 11, 13, annex A
Inadequate planning of the implementation — no analysis of implementation or allocation of related responsibilities	2, 3, 4, 5, 6, 11, annex C
Misapplication of *TUPE*	4
Poor relationship between contractor and the contract manager, especially if this person was once involved with preparing an in-house bid	5, 11
Inadequate split between purchaser and provider staff, resulting in conflicts of interest when dealing with in-house bids	5, 6
Unclear or imprecise roles, responsibilities and targets for effective teamworking	3, 4, 5, 6, 11
Possible loss of control over the facilities management function and ownership of, and access to, documents and knowledge	5
Lack of standard forms of facilities management contracts or inadequate conditions of contract	5
Inappropriate allocation of risks and rewards between college and service provider	5, 6, 14
Inadequate definition of the scope and content of services	7
Lack of consideration of all stakeholders in the facilities management sphere	7
Specifications are over-prescriptive and/or concentrate on procedures not outputs	7
Stakeholders 'gold plating' their requirements	7
Poorly controlled changes to user requirements	7, 11
Excessive monitoring of contractor performance	7

Risk	Chapter reference
Absence of, or poor system for, providing incentives for performance	7
Contract too inflexible to handle changes in user requirements during the contract and work outside specification	7
Failure to take account of relevant health and safety legislation at the correct time, leading to excessive cost later	8
Redundancy in the supply chain where cost is added without necessarily adding value	10
Poor bundling/grouping of activities to be contracted out	9
Absence of shared ownership of outcomes	10
Poor cashflow position for colleges and service providers	11
Financial failure of chosen service provider during contract period	11
Absence of benchmarks of cost and quality against which to measure performance and improvement	12
Lack of education and training in facilities management	13
Fraud or irregularities in the award and management of contracts	annex D

1.21 In pursuing more efficient and effective facilities management, colleges should also be aware of the opportunities that stem from a greater awareness of potential risks. To a large extent, the opportunities mirror the risks — as table 2 shows — acting as a counter to their influence.

Table 2. Opportunities arising from a greater awareness of potential risks

Risk	Chapter reference
Enhancing client capability and quality of provision, and proper assessment of requirements for the scope and content of services	3, 4
Identification and allocation of risks on a rational basis to help clarify relationships between contractors and facilities managers	3, 5, 9
Proper separation of duties between purchasers and providers	3, 5, 6
Clear responsibilities and targets for effective teamworking	3
Proper contract documentation with appropriate conditions of contract for both in-house and contracted-out services	7, 10, annex G, annex H
Proper allocation of risks and rewards	3, annex E
Improved response to customer and market requirements	2, 3
Improved performance with proper incentivisation	5, 6, 10, 11
Health and safety legislation incorporated into facilities management policies at the appropriate time	8
Shared ownership of outcomes	5, 6
Proper monitoring of contract performance	5, 6, 11
Improved cashflow forecasting and budgeting	2, 3
Opportunity to build up cost and quality benchmarks against which to measure performance and improvements	12
Properly focused education and training for in-house staff on facilities management matters	4, 6
Proper assessment of activities to be grouped/bundled for contracting out	6, 7
Efficiency gains enabling resources to be released for the improvement or expansion of curriculum provision	2

Conclusions

1.22 Colleges need to understand that they must be informed or intelligent clients in managing, amongst other things, their facilities. This requires a focus on service delivery which provides value for money and customer satisfaction in an environment in which risks abound. Effective facilities management comes from being able to devise and implement practices that reduce or eliminate the risks and which add value to the core business.

CHECKLIST

This checklist is intended to assist with the review and action planning processes.

		Yes	No	Action needed
a.	Does the importance of facilities management have a sufficiently high profile at the college?	☐	☐	☐
b.	Have college governors and the senior management team agreed a definition of facilities management?	☐	☐	☐
c.	Is the college able to determine whether or not it is achieving value for money in relation to its facilities management services, however provided?	☐	☐	☐
d.	Has the college considered its relationship with its service providers?	☐	☐	☐

Chapter 2

Developing Strategies for Facilities Management

Introduction

2.1   The starting point for managing facilities is the college business plan and accommodation strategy. These should be kept up to date and used to determine the nature and level of services support. This chapter reviews the approach to developing a facilities management strategy to reflect the college's business objectives, needs and policies, as well as the practicalities imposed by its accommodation. It will consider the successive stages in the process and show that a wide range of techniques and tools are at the disposal of a college's management to help them in their work.

Policy Considerations

2.2   The following key issues should be taken into consideration.

- the development of a facilities management strategy is a project in its own right and must be undertaken rigorously using appropriate techniques and tools

- colleges should follow three stages to produce an effective strategy for the management of their facilities:

    - **analysis stage** assembles all relevant facts including the college's objectives, needs and policies, a review of resources, processes, systems and the physical assets, together with their attributes in terms of space, function and utilisation

    - **solution stage** assembles the criteria for judging options, evaluating these against the objectives of the college, and develops the facilities management strategy

    - **implementation stage** completes the strategy development process through the establishment of an implementation plan which incorporates the key elements of procurement, training and, importantly, communication

- on completion, the facilities management strategy should relate closely to the college strategic plan and accommodation strategy. The facilities management strategy document should incorporate:

    - financial objectives

    - goals and critical success factors (in terms of time, cost and quality objectives)

- — targets for potential efficiency gains and quality improvements
- — customer-focus strategy
- — technical strategy
- — in-house/contracting-out strategy
- — procurement strategy
- — people plan
- — business processes
- — IT strategy.

- colleges need to see their facilities management strategy as the cornerstone of their accommodation strategy, not as an adjunct to it.

Guidance

Developing a Facilities Management Strategy

2.3   To manage facilities efficiently and effectively, robust strategies should be developed within the context of the college strategic plan and accommodation strategy. These should involve development of strategic objectives and a business plan for the facilities management function, with proper reference to the college's strategic plan, accommodation strategy and financial forecasts. A business plan for facilities management should:

- consider the needs of the college, differentiating between core and non-core business activities and identifying how these will be met

- establish effective and manageable processes for meeting the needs

- establish the appropriate resource needs for providing services, whether obtained internally or externally

- identify the source of funds to finance the strategy and its implications

- establish a budget not only for the short term, but also to achieve value for money over the long term

- recognise that management of information is key to providing a basis for effective control of facilities management.

2.4   This process of developing a facilities management strategy is illustrated in figure 1 which indicates the three main stages with their contributory elements.

Figure 1. Process of developing a facilities management strategy

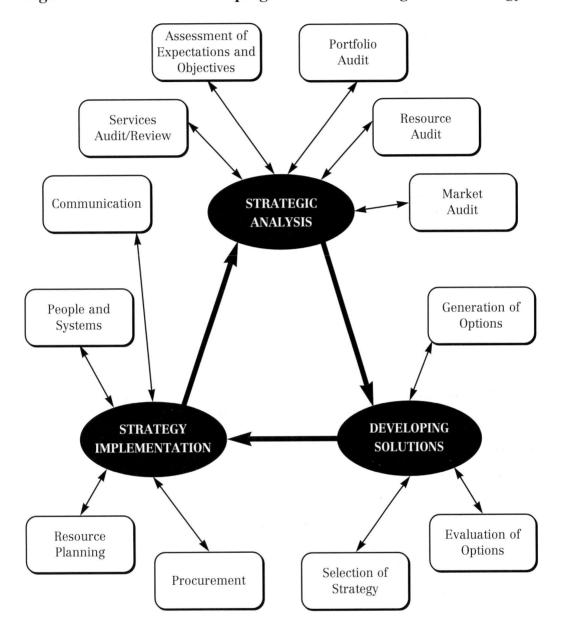

2.5 The three main stages in the development of a strategy are:

- strategic analysis

- developing solutions

- strategy implementation.

Table 3 presents possible management techniques and tools that are available.

Table 3. Techniques and tools to support development of a facilities management strategy

Development stage	Phase	Technique or tool
Strategic analysis	Services audit/review	Benchmarking
	Assessment of expectations and objectives	SWOT analysis
	Portfolio audit	Space analysis Property register Maintenance plan Risk audit
	Resource audit	People/skills' audit Service provider audit Process analysis
	Market audit	Service providers Property supply
Develop solutions	Generation of options	Outsource modelling Business process engineering (BPR)
	Evaluation of options	Maintenance plan Risk analysis Cost benefit analysis Feasibility/acceptability analysis
	Selection of strategy	Optimising model
Strategy implementation	People and systems	Change management through the application of rigorous project management (plan, monitor and control) Training and development BPR
	Organisation/structural implications	Effective communication Programmes
	Resource planning	Project planning/ programming/control
	Procurement	Service provider selection

Strategic Analysis of Facilities Requirements

2.6   The aim of the analysis is to establish a thorough understanding of the present state of the college's estates and facilities management. This means assembling all relevant facts, including:

- the college's objectives, needs and policies (from the college strategic plan)

- physical assets and space utilisation achieved (from the college's accommodation strategy)

- a review of resources, processes and systems to provide a broad picture of the current provision of services

- a cost analysis.

Assessment of expectations and objectives

2.7   Colleges should be able to define their expectations and objectives for their facilities. For instance, colleges might aspire to expand their core business into areas for which different kinds of facilities and services will be required to those currently provided. It would be useful, therefore, to broaden discussion to identify potential additions. These objectives should be embodied in a formal statement as part of the college's overall mission statement, or linked to it, and should relate to the college's business needs as found in its strategic plan.

Portfolio audit

2.8   Implicit in an audit of property and property-related assets will be the necessity for and provision of support services, maintenance plan(s) and an assessment of risks. Colleges will also need to consider their space utilisation and procedures for charging for the use of space. In itself, this kind of auditing will succeed in raising awareness of how space is being used and how economical that use is. Included in this audit must be an evaluation of the full cost of providing the space, that is, the costs of providing support services must form part of the exercise. This will help colleges establish which of their spaces are providing value for money and which are not.

Colleges must be constantly aware of the extent, quality and utilisation of their space and costs of providing it.

Room for improvement

CASE STUDY

The college had decided to audit its use of space and to establish a basis for charging departments for that use. When the figures were released, concerns were expressed by various departments. In one case, a department complained that its rooms were too small for the size and nature of its activities and that it might be forced to curtail some of them even though they were generating

additional revenue. In another case, a department felt that it was paying far too much for the space it had and was determined to seek a reduction. The substance of the complaint by the departmental head was that it was cheaper to rent commercial property in the town centre than pay for over-priced college rooms. These matters were resolved only after the principal was able to make an informed decision based on an up-to-date statement of the use of space, the need for space and the availability and cost of space elsewhere.

Market audit

2.9   Colleges should undertake a market audit periodically to establish the state of the property market (should acquisition become an option) and the position on service providers (see chapter 9). It is, however, likely that colleges will have this kind of information to hand from previous market audits carried out when preparing their accommodation strategy and from the valuation of their assets for financial accounting purposes.

Resource audit

2.10   Part of the strategic analysis should include a review of staff employed in the provision of services and facilities management. This will, of necessity, cover both in-house and contracted organisations. Additionally, colleges must analyse the processes that are contained within their facilities to determine, amongst other things, patterns of use and, with that, areas of intensive use. Colleges should critically review all existing human resources available to them, information about which should be available from their human resource planning (see chapter 4). The resource audit should concentrate on:

- **people** determine skills profiles and gaps

- **providers** determine capability, scope and terms of engagement

- **systems** establish the status of all procedures and technology by process analysis and systems' audit.

Services audit and review

2.11   Colleges should have also identified what their core and non-core business activities are. Differentiating between core and non-core business is necessary so that effort can be concentrated where it is most needed, that is, in developing the best learning, teaching and training environment. Typical of non-core business, apart from those mentioned in chapter 1, are catering, printing and conference facilities.

2.12   Colleges should critically review the operation of services provided. They should consider:

- **policy** by examining existing policies in terms of corporate guidelines and standards, performance standards, quality assurance, health and safety and other statutory requirements, human resources, financial and other approvals

Effective Facilities Management — A Good Practice Guide

- **process and procedures** by defining business processes including budgeting, procurement, purchasing approvals and payments

- **service delivery** by auditing all aspects of the estates management strategy and service delivery, including relationship with customers (especially cost, time and quality objectives).

2.13 In carrying out a review of the above aspects, colleges should make use of benchmarking (see chapter 12) as a method or tool for establishing current performance and achievement.

Developing Solutions

2.14 Once information from the analysis stage has been assembled, a robust and structured approach to the interpretation of the information should be adopted. It is essential that the interpretation of information derived from the analysis is open and allows new ideas and innovative solutions to be developed. The recommended approach comprises:

- assembling criteria for judging options

- evaluation of options

- selection of preferred option, that is, the college's *de facto* facilities management strategy.

2.15 Before any attempt is made to consider options, it is essential to identify and agree the criteria for judging them. Moreover, there needs to be a very clear separation between the assembly of criteria and their application to options.

2.16 The strategic analysis stage should have highlighted precisely how well the college's space and other attributes of its facilities match up to its needs. This means that options should be considered for bridging identified gaps as well as for bringing innovative solutions to present and future needs.

2.17 There are many ways in which colleges can establish options, for example, by consultation with stakeholders and invitations to external experts. All criteria must, however, include assessments of value for money and likely customer satisfaction.

2.18 At the conclusion of this stage, a facilities management strategy can be reflected in both the college's overall strategic plan and accommodation strategy. The strategy should reflect the following content:

- financial objectives

- goals and critical success factors (in terms of time, cost and quality objectives)

- targets for potential efficiency gains and quality improvements

- customer requirements

- technical issues

- risks

- in-house and contracting-out strategies (see chapter 3)

- human resource plan (see chapter 4)

- procurement strategy

- business processes

- support for IT strategy.

Strategy Implementation

2.19 Once established, broad policy statements should be developed into operational plans and implemented through a process that is capable of managing change. The change management process should be undertaken adopting best practice in human resources management (see chapter 4). The implementation plan should include timetables, milestones and proper risk management. The risks to successful implementation should be identified and responsibilities for managing these assigned (see annex C for an approach). The plan should encompass people and systems, communication, resource planning and procurement, each of which is discussed below.

People and systems

2.20 The most important phase in an implementation strategy is bringing about change in a controlled way. To achieve this, colleges need to develop people's skills and understanding so that they are fully conversant with the meaning and practice of facilities management. Education and training, together with the mentoring of individuals, will achieve these aims and enhance competence. Close monitoring and control of systems and procedures will help to ensure that these too develop in the ways intended. This is not a one-off exercise; there has to be a culture of continuous improvement with periodic checks on performance.

Communication

2.21 Effective communication between the college (as an informed or intelligent client) and service providers is essential to ensuring that the implementation of a strategy is both understood and acted upon (see chapters 4 and 5 and annex A). It is important to involve all stakeholders in the discussion about organisation and structure. Stakeholders are those people with a legitimate interest in a business or process, including staff, students, governors, statutory authorities, neighbours and the public to varying extents. Staff especially need to recognise that facilities management is an active process and, therefore, not one of simply reacting to problems as and when they arise. In organisational terms, this requires a structure which is flat so that staff, with decision-making abilities, are in close contact with customers to head off problems before they have the chance to develop.

Resource planning

2.22   Planning and controlling the use of resources in an efficient and effective manner is a job in its own right. Where colleges are large employers (of either in-house staff or external service providers), it makes good sense to plan for the optimum use of resources. When management teams are small and the demands on them appear modest, it is still necessary to take formal steps to plan resources. Even the best managers cannot keep everything in their heads. Information technology (IT) can help here through the use of low-cost project planning and scheduling software to help allocate resources to individual tasks and provide a means for measuring progress and performance.

Procurement

2.23   Finally, the point is reached where procurement of services can be considered and, as appropriate, partners can be selected (see chapters 3, 5, 6 and 10). The joint FEFC and NAO publication *Procurement: A Good Practice Guide* (FEFC/NAO 1997) gives practical information and guidance on the procurement process.

Relationships between Colleges and Service Providers

2.24   There will be changes of staff and other aspects of a college's management over time. Arrangements and agreements, with respect to facilities management, may well outlast the term of employment of key staff. It is important, therefore, that colleges recognise the need for:

- the purchaser, that is, the college, to be an informed or intelligent client

- a purchaser–provider relationship to develop between those commissioning the service and the service provider (both in house and contracted out).

2.25   In coming to terms with these needs colleges might benefit from a better understanding of the new tasks which this role as an informed or intelligent client represents (see annex A). This function will need a significant degree of operational knowledge and experience of not only the college's own business, but also of the service being provided.

2.26   The success of any change initiative in the delivery of services will depend on two main parties:

- the customer's (college's) representative (facilities manager, property manager)

- service providers, whether internal or external to the college.

2.27   Both parties need to share the common objective of delivering a value-for-money service. To be successful in achieving this goal, the interests of individuals within the two parties also need to be recognised. A co-operative approach, which recognises individuals' interests and aligns efforts with the goals of the college, has the potential to deliver the greatest benefit. A co-operative approach (for example, partnering) is also one of the recommended arrangements for managing external service providers (see chapter 10 and annex B; see also chapter 4 on human resources management implications).

Conclusions

2.28   Colleges need to see their facilities management strategy as the cornerstone of their accommodation strategy, not as an adjunct to it. By identifying the kind of accommodation and facilities currently provided and that required in the future, colleges will be able to quantify the gap that has to be bridged. There are, however, other aspects relating to facilities management that have to be considered carefully if the most appropriate strategy is to be developed. Various tools and techniques are available to support a rigorous process of analysis, solution development and implementation, success in which will lead to a workable strategy for effective facilities management.

CHECKLIST

This checklist is intended to assist with the review and action planning processes.

		Yes	No	Action needed
a.	Does the college accept the importance of a proper facilities management strategy within the context of the college strategic plan and accommodation strategy?	☐	☐	☐
b.	Has the college completed a strategic analysis of its facilities requirements?	☐	☐	☐
c.	Have new ideas and innovative solutions been considered in the context of facilities management strategy?	☐	☐	☐
d.	Has the broad strategy been developed into an operational plan addressing the issues of managing change?	☐	☐	☐
e.	Has the college considered its relationship with service providers?	☐	☐	☐

Chapter 3

Contract Out or Retain In House?

Introduction

3.1   This chapter considers the issue of whether or not to contract out services. Various options are available to colleges and have to be considered thoroughly if value for money (VFM) is to be maximised. The initial step for a college is to define its services requirements within an overall facilities management strategy. The next step is to consider the attributes of service which it sees as important. Finally, the college should be able to determine the mechanism through which service provision should take place. This decision is a significant one, which has many implications for the quality of service as well as its cost.

Policy Considerations

3.2   The following key issues should be taken into consideration.

- colleges must identify the key attributes of the services they require so that a balanced view of needs is established as the basis for evaluating available options as part of the decision to retain in house or contract out

- colleges should define their own evaluation criteria with respect to these attributes of service so that the importance or weight given to options is truly reflective of the college's accommodation and facilities management strategy and policies

- consideration must be given to both direct and indirect costs of service provision so that a complete financial picture is gained, with comparison made on a like-for-like basis to enable a decision to be taken on VFM grounds

- support services should represent the best VFM on the basis of affordability for the college in the implementation of the objectives of its strategic plan, irrespective of the cost of those services

- evaluation criteria for the sourcing decision must embrace hard and soft measures and compare all costs with the required quality

- roles and skills must be defined from the services to be provided, with specialist skills highlighted

- since the factors affecting the choice of in-house or contracted-out facilities management may change, the route by which services are procured should be reviewed at appropriate intervals.

Guidance

Attributes of Service

3.3   The attributes considered to be significant and/or important to colleges include, though are not limited to:

- customer service

- uniqueness of service

- priority, flexibility and speed of response

- management implications

- direct and indirect costs

- control.

Customer service

3.4   Colleges will have established the scope and standard of services required. In addition to the many 'hard' measures that are usually associated with this (for example speed of response), 'soft' measures must also be considered, for example the level of customer service. These might include:

- a responsive helpdesk in preference to a logbook in which faults are noted

- call-back to the customer to report that the work has been carried out

- adoption of performance measures for courtesy, presentation and tidiness.

Colleges need to have a helpdesk or central co-ordination point if they are to deal effectively with customer enquiries about facilities and related services.

When help is readily on hand

CASE STUDY

The college in question did not believe that, given its relatively small size, it warranted a helpdesk. After all, the estates manager seemed to know what was going on and he always seemed to be receiving calls from various people to tell him if there were problems. In fact, over a two-month period during the lead-up to Christmas, the estates manager was so overwhelmed with the number of calls and visits he received that he managed to do little other work. Moreover, there were complaints that some problems were not being addressed. In the end, he discussed the matter with the principal and persuaded him to allow a helpdesk to be set up on a three-month trial. Its scope was to cover security, transport, catering, cleaning, porterage, maintenance, mail services and room

bookings. In the first 10 days, the helpdesk attracted 500 enquiries of which all but a handful were dealt with promptly and to the satisfaction of the customer. In establishing the helpdesk, the college had created a focus for dealing with problems. This meant that staff were generally able to resolve problems there and then, rather than allowing them to fester.

3.5   In certain areas or during particular times of the day, the softer aspects may become more important and will require close attention — for example, dealing with members of the public, including prospective students, on open days or other occasions when they are newcomers to the college.

Uniqueness of service

3.6   When contemplating alternative means of service provision, the special demands of any service must be considered. Whilst most tasks will not represent an exception to providers within the industry, some exceptions are possible. For example, the college might possess specialist plant and equipment that are unfamiliar to maintenance operatives. This may restrict the potential choice of the provider of maintenance and supplier of spares. Issues may include:

- number of external suppliers that can potentially offer the service

- cost (premium) of the service

- average delivery time

- level of specification needed to place orders.

Priority, flexibility and speed of response

3.7   The priority of the service to be provided should be made clear, so that critical services can be highlighted and the required level of response taken into account. A risk assessment should be undertaken for high-priority services, so that the consequence of failures is made clear and the appropriate level and speed of response can be planned. This can be undertaken as follows:

- identify all sources of risk which might affect service provision

- undertake a preliminary analysis to establish the probable high-priority risks for further investigation

- examine these high-priority risks to assess the severity of their impact and probability of occurrence

- analyse all risks to predict the most likely outcome

- investigate alternative courses of action

- choose the course of action deemed necessary to hold, avoid, reduce, transfer or share risks, as appropriate

- allocate responsibility for managing risks — these should be placed with those who can best manage them.

3.8   A college's management team may use questionnaires and checklists to identify risks. High-priority services and their related risks must be identified and assessment made of the probability and consequences of such risks. Probabilities and consequences may be scored as shown in table 4.

Table 4. Risk scores

Probability

Improbable	10% chance of occurrence	1
Unlikely	25% chance	2
As likely as not	50% chance	3
Probable	75% chance	4
Highly probable	90% chance	5

Consequence

Insignificant	1
Marginal	2
Serious	3
Critical	4
Catastrophic	5

3.9   In most cases, it would be appropriate to add together the scores for probability and consequence to produce the total risk score. A score of 5 would be unacceptable and so the college would need to look at how such risks might be avoided, reduced or transferred. The value of this approach is that it enables risks to be recognised and assessed so that appropriate action can be taken. In the process of doing this, several risks impacting on services provision are able to be ranked to allow the college to look objectively at how they can be best managed.

3.10   For example, the occurrence of a significant failure in the heating system during the winter months might be improbable (score 1), but the consequences could be serious (score 3). The full impact of this risk is rated as 4 and is something which the college might be prepared to accept (hold). This can be contrasted with the 'as likely as not' event that fuel oil will not be delivered on time (score 3). If this were so, the consequences for heating the college could be serious (score 3). This gives a total score of 6. In other words, fuel oil deliveries are a high-priority service and, as such, must be made at the required time. The college should take steps to reduce the risk of non-delivery on specified dates. An alternative action would be to hold a greater quantity of fuel oil than is absolutely necessary, though this would raise costs as well as requiring larger storage tanks.

3.11   Colleges should also consider the level of flexibility required for each of the services provided. Variable demand for some services, such as porterage and transport which may peak at certain times of the year, can cause difficulties in maintaining a constant resource level. In such instances, the ability to call-off labour from an external provider at short notice can help and is also likely to provide a cost-effective way of delivering these services.

3.12   The speed with which a service provider can, under each service approach, respond to orders or requests is a factor for further consideration. For example, the response time of an external provider in the case of an emergency callout, may or may not be longer than an in-house resource. In the case of a remote campus, the response time for a maintenance contractor may be significant and a premium to reduce this time might prove prohibitive. Alternatively, if an emergency were to escalate, a large external provider may be preferred to the in-house alternative, because of ready access to necessary equipment and out-of-hours labour.

Management implications

3.13   The decision to contract out or provide services in house must take into account both the capability of service providers and the effort required to manage them. A college that takes the decision to contract out can delegate the direct supervision of work and service operatives to the provider. The role for the college's representative then becomes the management of the output from the service provider. The representative should act as an informed or intelligent client (see annex A) managing performance against specifications and service level agreements (see chapter 7). Colleges need to consider their approach to this new management role carefully.

3.14   In contemplating a mix of support services such as cleaning, security, building and mechanical and electrical maintenance, it is easy to see the diversity of tasks involved. This may mean that a manager or supervisor who is trying to cope with such a range of services may not be proficient in all. This could prove to be a problem for smaller colleges where the diversity of tasks is great, though not extensive, requiring the manager or supervisor to be multi-skilled. For larger colleges, specialist management and supervision may be cost effective and efficient, because more of it is required. A further consideration is that of the expertise available within the college for the management of these services if retained in house. Whilst accommodation services such as cleaning and porterage do not require high levels of expertise, statutory equipment testing and maintenance of major appliances do. For a manager whose remit includes the management of such services on a part-time basis, the initial learning and the continuing professional development, to keep abreast of legislation and industry practice, represents a significant investment in time and effort. Consequently, in-house service providers may not be the most cost-effective choice.

Direct and indirect costs

3.15   In choosing the approach to service provision, the total cost of provision is the one most often mis-reported. In evaluating the comparative cost between in-house or contracted-out service provision, colleges should identify all costs, both direct and indirect. A common mistake is for only the direct costs to be reported. In the case of contracted-out provision, the contract sum is a clear, direct cost that is readily available. However, the internal management cost should also be included. For in-house provision, the cost calculation should include not only the more obvious cost of employment including benefits and so on of those direct staff, but also their on-going training and development. Furthermore, the full administration of the services such as permit-to-work procedures, competent and approved person regimes, together with the technology to operate them, all attract a cost which must be recorded.

3.16   Colleges also need to consider the costs of financial administration. For instance, a small number of labour and material contracts means that invoices can be processed at a more effective cost compared to situations in which invoices are many and frequent. Clearly, the method of procurement has an implication for the accounting function, although the number of invoices generated is unlikely to reduce below a particular level in cases where multiple suppliers complement direct labour.

Control

3.17   Linked closely to the management variable is the issue of control. For many colleges considering contracting out, the greatest concern is that of a perceived loss of control. The level of control which can be achieved is closely correlated with the method of procurement and the contractual relationship established between the college and service provider. Through a more traditional contract the level of control is limited. For more control, a partnering arrangement may be appropriate (see chapter 10).

3.18   Whatever arrangement is put in place, technology has a part to play in the delivery of reliable management information. It is through available and accessible management information that many of the control issues can be solved. In so doing, value can also be added if the management information is delivered as a consequence of service provision and is therefore available without cost or, at least, for a nominal sum.

Overview of Options and Implications

3.19   There are several options which a college can consider: it is not simply a choice between in-house provision or contracting out. Table 5 shows six options (defined in table 6) which a college might consider.

Table 5. Illustration of options and their implications

Attributes of service of importance to the college	In-house	Special company	Managing agent	Managing contractor	Total FM	Off the shelf/ agency
Customer service	+	+	++	+	+	−
Uniqueness of service	−	+	+	+	+	−
Control	++	++	++	+	−	+
Direct cost	+	−	−	−	−	−
Priority/flexibility/ speed of response	++	+	++	++	+	++
Management implications/ indirect cost	−	+	+	+	++	−

Note: ++ most likely to be satisfied; + may be satisfied; – unlikely to be satisfied adequately

Table 6. Definition of options

In-house
This option consists of the retention of the college's staff for the delivery of facilities services.

Special company
This option consists of the reconstitution of the in-house team into an independent company, with the objective of expanding its business by gaining contracts for other clients.

Managing agent
This option consists of the appointment of a specialist to act as client representative. This person (or organisation) is then responsible for arranging the appointments of service providers.

Managing contractor
This is where an organisation is appointed to manage all service providers as though they are part of one large contracting organisation. The contractor is paid a fee for providing this service.

Total facilities management (total FM)
The responsibility for providing services and for generally managing the facilities is placed in the hands of a single organisation.

Off-the-shelf/agency
This refers to the process of the contractual employment of staff through a specialist or general recruitment agency. Agencies provide variable standards of selection expertise, staff support and training and customer support.

3.20 Table 5 shows how the different attributes of services of importance to the college can be scored against each option. The particular interpretation represented by this model is a hypothetical one based on the authors' experiences. Moreover, it should be used only at the early stages, when determining an approach to the overall provision of services. Many of the attributes listed will, at a later stage, be used in the assessment of tenders.

3.21 Colleges should always consider their own evaluation criteria to determine the importance or weight which might be given to an option in terms of its potential to add value to the core business. Although signs are used in the example based on the authors' perceptions and experience, a numerical system could have been used to arrive at similar, if not the same, answers. Whichever approach is adopted, the basis for each score must be made explicit so that there can be no misunderstanding of the relative weighting of attributes. Furthermore, the exact interpretation of options will differ from one college to another, but the adoption of such an approach should enable objective comparison to be made and for it to be transparent to all stakeholders.

Market Testing

3.22 Even when services are retained in house, it is important to have the in-house provider(s) competing for the work alongside external contractors. Such exercises should take account of the resources and costs involved, not just for the college but for service providers. Going to the market should be an honest attempt at establishing the attraction or otherwise of contracting out. This does not, however, imply frequent tendering exercises. Appropriate arrangements would include regular comparisons of current prices and rates for services using published data, participation in a benchmarking club (see chapter 12) or indicative quotations from potential service providers. Colleges should, therefore, be aware of the state of the market for services. This is necessary so that at any time a college can judge whether or not a preferred option is the most appropriate. It is possible that colleges will have certain information from market audits when carried out during the preparation of their accommodation strategy. It will be necessary, however, for that information to identify whether or not there are sufficient suppliers who can meet colleges' needs.

3.23 Should a college decide to contract out, it is then faced with a further decision as to how the contracting out will be organised and structured. How will the contracts be let? Will there be separate or bundled individual contracts, a total facilities management package or a management contract (see chapter 9)? If the last option is exercised, the college will need to consider whether this should be undertaken for a fee or on the basis of service performance.

3.24 In most cases, it will be sufficient for colleges to review the decision to contract out every 12 months, though the exact period will vary according to the services involved and any existing conditions of contract. Colleges should try to avoid letting contracts on less than an annual basis. This can add to cost, as well as limiting the performance of the service provider. Annual reviews should, however, be incorporated into contracts running over two or more years. In all cases, the performance of service providers will form part of the assessment at an annual review. The mechanisms for this are dealt with in chapters 7 and 11.

Conclusions

3.25 The decision to contract out should be made on a rational and objective basis. At any time, colleges can apply the evaluation model shown in table 5 to help determine whether or not to contract out a service. The benefit in using a model of this kind is that specific options can be evaluated with sensitivity and that the correct decision for the college at any one time can be made. Time is an important factor, since needs change and sometimes the most appropriate option is the one that can be adapted over time to suit new circumstances. Colleges can effectively allow the market to make the decision for it by conducting periodic market testing exercises in which in-house providers compete for work alongside external contractors. There will be advantages and disadvantages to providing services either in house or by contracting out. The college must decide the route that provides the best VFM for itself in the long term. This is achieved by taking full account of the implications, especially the costs of all options.

CHECKLIST This checklist is intended to assist with the review and action planning processes.

		Yes	No	Action needed
a.	Has the college established the scope and standard of customer services required and compared it to its current provision of facilities management services?	☐	☐	☐
b.	Do the college's current facilities management arrangements properly address priorities and provide flexibility and speed of response?	☐	☐	☐
c.	Has the college considered the management implications of contracting out services as opposed to retaining them in house?	☐	☐	☐
d.	Has the college properly identified both the direct and indirect costs of service provision?	☐	☐	☐
e.	Has the level of control required been properly integrated with the methods of procurement and the contractual relationships that might be established between the college and the service provider?	☐	☐	☐
f.	Has the college put in place arrangements for regularly market testing services?	☐	☐	☐

Chapter 4

Human Resources Management Implications

Introduction

4.1   Adopting any significant change in the way in which estate-related services are provided will certainly have an impact on the culture of the college and the nature of relationships with both internal and external parties. This chapter highlights those aspects of human resources management (HRM) that need to be addressed when developing a strategy to improve the value of support services required by the college.

Policy Considerations

4.2   The following key issues should be taken into consideration.

- human resources management (HRM) issues need to be considered during the development of the college's strategic plan and accommodation strategy as an integral part of managing the provision of its support services and facilities

- senior management's goal of achieving VFM for the college needs to be shared by all staff

- significant changes in the extent of contracting out will have an impact on the roles and responsibilities of those concerned, requiring changes to HRM policy and procedures

- the college must make clear its position on *TUPE (Transfer of Undertakings (Protection of Employment) Regulations 1981)*, if it is to have the confidence of its workforce. Moreover, colleges must establish how *TUPE* affects their policies, procedures and actions to ensure that they comply with the legislation.

Guidance

Impact of Changes

4.3   The need for changes in the college's current HRM practices will depend upon the extent to which in-house services are to be contracted out to external service providers, as well as the type of policies and practices that are currently in place. Some colleges will have already considered many of the issues highlighted in this guidance. The sections that follow effectively act as a check against the main aspects of HRM that need to be reviewed if change is being considered.

Appropriate Management Structure

4.4   Any significant change in the number of services that are contracted out will have an impact on the structure of the department or organisation; in the case of contracting out all estate-related services, a small core management team is required to control and co-ordinate the activities of the external parties. In this instance, the role of management changes from direct or hands-on management to the management of the output of others, that is, the performance measurement of deliverables. The main management tasks then become the contract management of the respective contracts and the definition and development of policy and procedures. In this connection, it is essential to ensure that there is a split between purchaser and provider, regardless of whether or not services are contracted out, with the purchaser acting as the intelligent client in order to monitor the performance of in-house service delivery. These policies and procedures, along with relevant standards, are vital if the respective contracts are to meet the expectations of customers and are not to encourage malpractice or some other kind of irregularity.

4.5   The most appropriate management structure will be the one that ensures both control and economy for the college over its facilities. This means that colleges will need to determine exactly the number of staff and their functions for managing the provision of services, whether they are contracted out or retained in house. In the study of value for money, many colleges saw the need to retain their management teams at levels similar to those already present, even if they moved entirely to a contracted-out scenario. Clearly, the management of contractors is different from the supervision of directly employed staff, but this should not demand as high a level of resources. It is acceptable that some staff will have to be retained even where the college has opted for total facilities management by a single contractor (see chapter 9) since the informed or intelligent client function (ICF) must be maintained (see annex A). Under these circumstances, the need is for someone to be able to manage the college–contractor interface. The duties involved here can be summarised as:

- maintaining and enhancing the ICF

- defining property-related and space standard policies and monitoring space utilisation

- understanding customer requirements and keeping customers up to date

- planning projects involving new or additional works

- managing the approvals process and payments to the contractor

- measuring the performance of the contractor.

Employment Obligations

4.6   Employment obligations, both legal and moral, need to be carefully considered before contracting out. The *Transfer of Undertakings (Protection of Employment) Regulations 1981* (*TUPE*) stipulate that, in the case of directly employed staff, there should be a consultation period before services are contracted out. In the case of contract staff, colleges should pass details of their staff to the firms tendering for the contracts. The scope of *TUPE* extends to cover all subsequent situations where the employment status of staff is subject to change. It is essential, therefore, for colleges to establish how *TUPE* affects their policies, procedures and actions to ensure that they comply with the legislation.

4.7   The obligation to consult staff is an obligation to consult with elected representatives of the employees, or with any recognised trade union. If there are no recognised trade unions and no elected representatives, the employer is under a duty to procure the election of representatives. It is not only representatives of staff who may be transferred who must be consulted, but also representatives of any staff who may be affected by the transfer. The duty to inform and consult is, therefore, very broad. The information which must be passed to the employee includes what measures the transferee (that is, the new contractor) intends to take with regard to their employment.

4.8   This is a complex area of legislation and specialist advice should be sought. Consideration should be given to both the organisation of the process as well as the inclusion, within tendering documentation, of necessary clauses. This is required so that the mechanism by which *TUPE* operates can then be put in place. In cases where *TUPE* does not apply, a redundancy situation may arise, and different procedures will have to be observed (and, of course, selection for redundancy must be fair).

Functions, Job Descriptions and Skills

4.9   As changes occur in the mode of managing facilities, it is likely that the functions required to be performed will also change. This will mean that job descriptions have to be revised for those with responsibility for managing services. The content of these revised job descriptions will dictate the selection of appropriate individuals for positions. In assigning individuals to positions that require interaction with service providers, including in-house teams, an understanding of operations and performance issues will be required, as well as strong inter-personal skills and a knowledge of contracts.

4.10   All job descriptions should incorporate a means for evaluating the performance of staff. It is important that job descriptions are accompanied by role evaluation procedures so that staff and management are aware from the outset as to what is expected.

Colleges must be prepared to invest in their people, by providing them with opportunities to retrain for new roles and responsibilities.

It's people who count

 **CASE STUDY**

When a large college on a city centre campus decided to completely overhaul its facilities management, it was faced with some tough choices: attempt to make everyone redundant and start over again; transfer everyone on the payroll to a new service provider; or invest in the retraining and reskilling of the workforce. After much discussion behind the scenes, it was agreed that it would be more prudent, at least at this time, to opt for retraining and reskilling. There were many cynics, not only on the college management but also amongst the workforce. For them, it was a case of having 'heard it all before'. Undeterred, the newly appointed facilities manager decided to take the matter into her own hands. First, there were awareness seminars at which everything was brought out into the open. Next, the workforce was regrouped and refocused on its new challenges and goals. Finally, a permanent communications centre was established and charged with the responsibility of making everything in the facilities directorate, as it was now known, much more visible for everyone. A regular newsletter is now published and distributed to college staff and students. The college has since adopted the Investors in People (IiP) standards to help strengthen its links with training and development. The college will soon be ready for self-assessment.

4.11 The issues highlighted in this guidance will introduce new ways of operating in a number of areas. These may require managers to develop existing skills further or to learn new skills in order to implement changes effectively. In particular, introducing new information management procedures and systems will require additional training. Difficulties can arise because of the need for staff to adjust to new working practices. Handled sensitively, colleges should be able to overcome problems that might arise, through briefings, seminars and external training programmes (see chapter 13).

4.12 Managers also need to be aware of the prevailing market for estate-related and facilities services and what is required to manage service providers effectively. The management staff who deal directly with service providers need different skills to those in a direct line management position. This should be recognised so that training and development needs can be identified (see chapter 13).

Performance Appraisal

4.13 Management at all levels should be subject to performance appraisal, including those managers who either work for or are part of a service provider organisation. The assessment of the performance of service providers in particular is discussed in chapter 7. Customer representatives (facilities managers or property managers) who deal with service providers should be set performance objectives which reflect the management relationship with those service providers, along with the actions taken to monitor the performance and deal with any shortcomings. This could, for example, take the form of targets for tasks planned and completed over a given period, percentage of response times met and number of tasks requiring to be reworked. Where performance depends on the efforts of a group of people, performance at the group level should also be addressed through either the individual's appraisal or at group sessions.

Conclusions

4.14   HRM is a sensitive area for all organisations including colleges. Increasing legislation has added to the burden on colleges to have clear policies and procedures in place, no more so perhaps than in the case of *TUPE*. These have to be complete and apply regardless of whether or not a service is contracted out or retained in house. Colleges need to adopt a management structure that is appropriate to the mode of service provision and understand their obligations as employers. Job descriptions and skill requirements must be made explicit and procedures put in place to appraise and reward performance against measurable outputs or outcomes.

CHECKLIST

This checklist is intended to assist with the review and action planning processes.

		Yes	No	Action needed
a.	Is the college's management structure appropriate to the delivery of cost-effective and efficient management services?	☐	☐	☐
b.	Have job functions, job descriptions and service requirements been properly described in relation to the provision of management services?	☐	☐	☐
c.	Are the college's staff involved in delivering job functions, job descriptions and service requirements?	☐	☐	☐
d.	Is an appropriate method of performance appraisal in place?	☐	☐	☐
e.	Do the current arrangements properly recognise employment obligations and in particular the *Transfer of Undertakings Protection of Employment Regulations 1981 (TUPE)*?	☐	☐	☐

Chapter 5

Policy and Procedures for Contracting Out

Introduction

5.1   This chapter provides guidance on the procurement of works, supplies and services — referred to collectively as services — where the decision to contract out has been reached. In addition, this guidance applies to situations where currently contracted-out services are being re-tendered and/or rationalised.

5.2   For clarity, the guidance follows the process in chronological order as far as practicable. The objective is to ensure that the following critical success factors are achieved:

- the scope of the services and interfaces with related services are defined

- the service level required by stakeholders from the contracted-out provider(s) is clearly defined

- the contracted-out provider has the capabilities and skills to deliver the service

- internal departments and students are recognised as customers and treated as such

- service provision is provided through a team approach, with each member working towards a common goal

- service provision is continually reviewed and improved.

Policy Considerations

5.3   The following key issues should be taken into consideration.

- there is a logical sequence to contracting out services. This covers strategy, tender documentation, tendering and contract award. A realistic timescale must be allowed if the overall process is to be successful

- contracting out involves many activities and these have to be managed. A detailed programme should be prepared to help manage the process and to keep all interested parties informed

- defining the scope of services is crucial to successful contracting out. This provides the basis for inviting tenders and administering the contract. A poorly defined scope will lead, almost inevitably, to problems in the management of the service

- all stakeholders must be involved in the process of contracting out if their needs, as well as those identified in the facilities management strategy, are to be fully addressed and communicated. Success depends on all who could possibly contribute committing themselves to the process.

Guidance

Overview

5.4   Further information on procurement is provided in *Estate Management in Further Education Colleges: A Good Practice Guide* (FEFC/NAO 1996) which contains guidance on the subject of contracting out, though not explicitly to services contracts. A second publication in this Good Practice Guide series, *Procurement* (FEFC/NAO 1997) offers practical advice on the selection and evaluation of suppliers and tendering procedures. Additionally, colleges may refer to chapter 1 of the current guide on the risks encountered in contracting out and to annex E which provides an effective checklist. Colleges should consider addressing risk assessment and risk transfer as part of the process for procuring services. This will mean that risk assessment forms part of the policy and procedures for contracting out. Guidance on risk assessment is given in chapter 3.

5.5   To illustrate the contracting-out process, a generic procurement programme is set out below, with each activity subsequently described in more detail. Figure 2 outlines the main activities in the procurement of services. Its aim is to provide an indication of the order and timescales involved in moving from the definition of the services required by the college to those services actually being provided within the college. It is grouped into three main stages:

- **strategy**   covering the definition of services, current arrangements, the position of stakeholders and legislation affecting employment and procurement

- **tender documents**   covering service specifications, service level agreements and conditions of contract

- **tendering process**   covering tender briefing and assessment, contract award, pre-contract meeting, mobilisation and review.

5.6   The timescales will vary according to the scope and scale of services being contracted out. However, many of the critical periods, for instance dealing with legislative aspects, contractual matters, tenderers' briefing, tender period and mobilisation, will remain more or less the same for a wide range of contract types and values. The timescale might reduce for activities such as the definition of services, current arrangements, identifying stakeholders, tender assessment and contract award, where the service to be contracted out is of minor economic importance and uncomplicated. As with any exercise of this kind, it is easy to underestimate the time taken to move from the decision to contract out, to the start of the service.

Figure 2. Activities in the procurement of services

Activity/Months	1	2	3	4	5	6	7	8	9	10	11	12
Strategy												
Defining services	■											
Current arrangements	■											
Identifying stakeholders	■											
Employment legislation	■	■	■	■								
Tender Documents												
Service specifications	■											
Service level agreement		■										
Conditions of contract		■										
Tendering Process												
Tenderer briefing		■										
Tendering period			■									
Tender assessment				■								
Pre-contract meeting					■							
Contract award					■							
Mobilisation of resources						■						
Review of performance									■			■

Strategy

Defining services

5.7   It is critical to the success of any contracting-out process that all required services, including interfaces, are clearly defined (see also chapter 2). For example, are services such as pest control, waste disposal and sanitary services to be part of the cleaning contract? Such definition is required to ensure that all necessary services are provided and that no gaps exist between the interfaces of each service.

Services must have their scope clearly defined, with special attention paid to instances where some services can potentially fall in the gaps between service contracts.

Someone must be responsible

CASE STUDY

When infestation of the ceiling void above the kitchens was discovered, the immediate reaction was to call in the cleaning contractor. After all, the contractor was responsible for removal of waste and related duties. In the event, the contractor pointed out that any occurrence of this kind was not his responsibility. The contractor appeared to have acted correctly, but there was the understanding, at least in the mind of the estates manager, that matters like the one encountered were included in the scope of the cleaning contract. The outcome was that the college agreed to pay the contractor to remove the infestation and then formally instructed that the revised scope be included within the contract. Fortunately for the college, the service contract contained provision for changes of this kind to be made.

Current arrangements

5.8   The following base information should be collated in relation to current services prior to the initiation of the contracting-out process:

In-house services

   •   number of employees

   •   employment details: age, starting date, length of service, experience, special skills, salary and benefits

   •   equipment inventory.

Contracted-out services

   •   contract expiry date

   •   contract value

   •   scope of existing services and special demands.

Identifying stakeholders

5.9   Stakeholders are those parties with an interest in the services to be provided, such as internal and external customers. To secure the success of the process, it is important that they are identified and their requirements understood, with specifications and service levels aligned to their needs (see chapter 7). Whilst it may not always be possible, given the constraints that may be imposed on the in-house team to satisfy all specific requirements, they can be ranked according to their benefit to the business to ensure that the more significant ones are met.

5.10   Essentially, any individual or organisation with a legitimate interest in the college is a stakeholder. They include:

- students

- college staff

- service providers and suppliers

- college governors

- neighbours

- statutory authorities

- FEFC and NAO

- the general public.

Employment and public procurement legislation

5.11   Before proceeding with the re-tender or contracting out of services, it is essential to consider the implications of current employment and procurement legislation (see chapters 4 and 8). As regards the former, the relevant legislation is the *Transfer of Undertakings (Protection of Employment) Regulations 1981* (*TUPE*). At present these regulations protect the contracts of employment of both directly employed staff and the contractor's staff where the service has already been contracted out.

5.12   In relation to directly employed staff, the college's obligations are more onerous and will usually involve a consultation period with employees. Where contractor's staff are involved, the college will usually only be involved in communicating employee details to the tendering companies (see chapter 4).

5.13   New precedents are continually being set by the courts in relation to this area of legislation, for example in the definition of a full-time employee. It is, therefore, important and prudent to seek professional advice on the specific implications for each service that is contracted out.

5.14   In addition to the above, the implications of the *Public Works, Supply and Services Contract Regulations 1995* must also be considered. The main principle behind this legislation is to ensure that for service contracts above a specified threshold:

- specifications are non-discriminatory

- firms and individuals are selected objectively for inclusion in tender lists

- the tender process is transparent.

5.15   Colleges are required by EC public procurement directives to publish the tender for the provision of supplies, services and works over a certain value in the *Official Journal of the European Communities* (*OJEC*). The contract value thresholds, above which tenders should appear in the *OJEC*, are as follows:

- supplies and services   £158,018

- works   £3,950,456.

5.16   The above values were correct at May 1997, and they are reviewed every two years. An annual 'periodic indicative notice' is required, covering each priority service category on which it is expected that more than £592,568 (valid until December 1997) will be spent. Colleges should check these limits and, thus, the requirement to advertise in the *OJEC* before inviting tenders. Total contract value, regardless of contract period, is the basis of assessment, not annual cost. This requirement has been seen by some organisations as something which they might circumvent. It is not unknown for organisations to reduce the size of contracts by breaking them into smaller parts, thus reducing their size to below the threshold. Such practices are effectively outlawed by the EC. Colleges should take appropriate legal advice and verify the position on public procurement procedures as legislation can change.

5.17   Responsibilities should also be clearly split between procurement and provider staff when in-house tenders are sought in addition to those from external service providers. This will avoid conflicts of interest which might otherwise arise when subsequently assessing tenders.

Tender Documents

Service specifications

5.18   A service specification quantifies the acceptable standard of service required by the customer and will generally form a part of the contract with the service provider (see chapter 7). Its production is a prerequisite for drafting a service level agreement (SLA). Specifications set out standards covering college policy, department requirements, statutory requirements, health and safety standards and manufacturers' recommendations. The specification may also outline the procedures needed to achieve required technical standards.

Service level agreement

5.19   This builds on the service specification by amplifying, in practical terms, the obligations of each party. Technical and quality standards will usually be defined in relation to industry standards or manufacturer's recommendations, whereas performance will be related to the specific requirements of stakeholders, that is, frequency of activity and response times to callouts (see chapter 7). This agreement need only include, at the tendering stage, a framework setting out the overall performance parameters with detailed procedural issues to be evolved and refined during the life of the contract. Whilst the scope must be made clear, detailed day-to-day operating procedures can only be honed as the knowledge and experience of each service partner is built up over time. SLAs must be kept up to date.

Conditions of contract

5.20   Wherever possible, it is recommended that industry standard contracts are used to formalise legal relationships between the college and contractors. Standard forms of contract may be obtained from a number of sources which include:

- **Joint Contracts Tribunal (JCT)**   building contracts, maintenance and small works

- **Chartered Institute of Purchasing and Supply**   facilities management model agreement for service contracts, cleaning, security and so on.

Lack of standard forms of facilities management contracts or inadequate conditions of contract can lead to serious difficulties.

A matter of bad form

CASE STUDY

In negotiating contracts with suppliers and service providers, it is essential to ensure that the client's position is properly protected and not compromised. Legal advice should be sought in these matters. In one case, a college entered into a contract with a service provider only to find later that the terms and conditions were biased in the contractor's favour. The college did not have access to any standard form of contract and, therefore, accepted the contract as drafted by the service provider (the contractor) who was, after all, an established and respected company. A clause in the contract held the college liable for redundancy payments if any of the staff employed by the contractor had to be made redundant following a decline in use of certain of the facilities. Subsequently, there was a fall in the use of the particular facility and the college had to make substantial payments.

5.21   Any amendments required to these forms of contract should be clearly stated in the tender documents. Normally, it should not be necessary to amend standard conditions, as to do so might lead to unforeseen events and consequences. If colleges wish to amend standard forms, legal advice should be sought.

5.22   The purpose of forms of contracts is to provide the formal, legally binding framework within which service specifications and SLAs can operate. As such, they should not attempt to restate the contents of specifications and SLAs. Annex F contains useful guidance on contractual approaches and terms. Additionally, the Central Unit on

Procurement (CUP) *Guidance Note 42, Contracting for the Provision of Services*, outlines the possible contents and structure of a service contract.

5.23   An important consideration, in terms of contract conditions, is that they should allow for changes to be made as experience of operating a contract grows. SLAs will be kept up to date and, therefore, a contract that was so inflexible as to prevent changes would represent an unworkable arrangement. Contracts should be seen, therefore, not as strait-jackets, but as frameworks within which to operate and develop good practice. As a minimum, contracts should contain clauses which allow for changes to be made to the provision of services, so long as they are not so significant as to alter the overall the scope and content of the contract. These clauses should also cover the mechanism for adjusting the contract sum in the event of changes being required by the college.

Tendering Process

Tender briefing

5.24   Depending on the complexity of the services being tendered, it is often useful to organise a tenderers' briefing during the tender period. This can be either formal or informal so long as the latter is conducted on a consistent basis for all tenderers. The object of this briefing would be to:

- show companies the facilities

- explain the principles of the contract

- clarify the requirements of the tender submission

- answer any questions that may arise.

5.25   In the course of these briefings, it is important to advise tenderers that lowest price will not be the sole factor in choosing between tenders: quality of service will be taken into account. Care must also be exercised in conducting such briefings in order to avoid collusion between parties or allegations that one party is being treated more favourably than others (see annex D).

Tender period

5.26   Where the value of services to be tendered exceeds the EC public procurement thresholds (see paragraph 5.15) the tender period must comply with the duration set out in the regulations. In any event, it is good practice to allow sufficient time for tenderers to consider fully the documentation and allow them to submit a considered proposal. This should never be fewer than two weeks from receipt of documents.

Tender assessment

5.27   Colleges should allow themselves sufficient time to assess tenders. Assessment criteria should be agreed in advance in relation to technical, quality of service and resource requirements and these may also be incorporated in the tender documents.

These should then be applied to each tender submission in order to shortlist companies for interview, perhaps requiring them to make a formal presentation. Additionally, inspection of a company's premises and order books could provide valuable insights into its ability to meet the demands of the new contract. A major consideration is whether or not a company is able physically to perform the service for the tender price. Colleges should inquire as to the credit-worthiness of shortlisted companies and require contact names of existing clients from whom performance references might be obtained.

5.28   The concept of least whole-term cost should be used to evaluate tenders commercially. Least whole-term cost takes into account the cost of the services over the duration of the contract, that is, including annual price fluctuations, lifecycle cost issues, payback on capital investment and so on. In other words, it is a matter of determining the total cost of each tender, enabling comparison on a like-for-like basis.

Practical steps to weighing cost and quality

5.29   Lowest price is not the sole factor in deciding which tender to accept, although tenders are mostly accepted on the basis of price. Quality should play an equal part in any evaluation if value for money is to mean anything. For some contracts it may be difficult to determine the quality of service: rarely can quality or performance be considered in absolute terms. It is possible to take account of quality by judging it against benchmarks established in service specifications or other objective measures. *Estate Management in Further Education Colleges: A Good Practice Guide* (FEFC/ NAO 1996) provides clear guidance on tender assessment with regard to value and other qualitative criteria (see also tables 5 and 6 on p.27).

5.30   There are other ways in which cost and quality may be judged. For instance, in the case of professional services, one approach would be to operate a two-envelope tender system. Short-listed consultants are sent model agreements and asked to submit a lump sum tender, along with their time charges for extra work. The first tender describes the quality of service to be provided, the second gives the price. Two separate panels look at the tenders.

5.31   A quality panel of, say, four people is convened to rank the tenderers A, B and C, according to the quality which they believe each tenderer represents. The panel applies a percentage adjustment (or weighting) to the services offered by each: it is necessary that all panellists agree. Once the quality panel has finished its deliberations, the price panel opens the envelopes containing the price tenders. The decision is then taken to award the contract to the consultant offering the highest quality at the lowest price, based on a simple calculation.

Contract award, pre-contract meetings, mobilisation and review

5.32   Following the selection of the best tender and award of the contract, a pre-contract meeting should be called to address the following issues:

- service provider's programme for start and provision of the service

- insurance details

- contract administration, that is, payments and meetings.

5.33 The contractor should be given a sufficient mobilisation period to marshal all resources, thus ensuring a seamless continuation of service provision. Where the service(s) affected are to be contracted out for the first time, it would be useful to have the contractor visit the college to explain to users of the service what is expected of them. During this period, it will be necessary to plan for the regular review of the service provider's performance. The frequency of revisions will depend on the duration and complexity of the contract. Typically, three-monthly reviews would be reasonable, though monthly reviews during the early stages might be more appropriate in order to deal with teething problems.

Ongoing Relationships

5.34 The relationship between the contractor and the college's representative is a crucial one in ensuring that the service is provided as expected. Moreover, colleges will want to improve the level of performance over time, so sound working relationships are important. This can, however, be one of those areas where problems can arise and which effectively sour the relationship.

5.35 One example is where the person occupying the role of representative is also the person who prepared the unsuccessful in-house tender. Colleges should, therefore, be prepared to make changes to their management, if necessary, to ensure that poor working relationships do not arise as a consequence of earlier decisions.

Conclusions

5.36 Colleges need to recognise that successful contracting out of estate-related services comes from a process in which policies are clearly defined and procedures are progressive and transparent. All of this takes time and so colleges must plan well ahead before embarking on a contracting-out route. If followed carefully, procedures that lead to contracting out can provide a firm basis for the subsequent management and administration of contracts.

CHECKLIST | **This checklist is intended to assist with the review and action planning processes.**

		Yes	No	Action needed
a.	Has the base information in relation to current services prior to the initiation of the contracting-out process been properly correlated?	☐	☐	☐
b.	Have the stakeholders with an interest in the services to be provided been properly identified and consulted?	☐	☐	☐
c.	Have the services to be contracted out been clearly identified and defined?	☐	☐	☐
d.	Does the college properly understand the implications of relevant employment and public procurement legislation?	☐	☐	☐
e.	Do the tender documents include full service specifications, the terms of proposed service level agreement and conditions of contract?	☐	☐	☐
f.	Is the tender process sufficiently rigorous to allow for proper competition?	☐	☐	☐
g.	Are proper tender evaluation procedures in place?	☐	☐	☐
h.	Is the process of tender and contract award properly addressed in the strategy?	☐	☐	☐
i.	Are arrangements in place to ensure ongoing relationships between the contractor and the college?	☐	☐	☐

Chapter 6

Policy and Procedures for In-house Provision

Introduction

6.1   This chapter provides good practice guidance for the establishment of policy and procedures to be adopted where services are provided in house. For clarity, the guidance has been set out to follow the process in chronological order.

6.2   The objective of this guidance is to ensure that the following critical success factors are met:

- scope of the services and interfaces with related services are defined
- the service level required by stakeholders from the in-house team is clearly defined
- the in-house team has the capabilities and skills to deliver the service
- internal departments and students are recognised as customers and treated as such
- in-house service provision is provided through a team approach, with each member working towards a common goal
- service provision is continually reviewed and improved.

Policy Considerations

6.3   The following key issues should be taken into consideration.

- defining the scope of a service is as important to successful in-house provision as it is to contracting out. A poorly defined scope will lead, almost inevitably, to problems in the management of the service with higher supervision costs and a lowering of customer satisfaction
- colleges must establish the extent of the knowledge and skills which their staff possess. Where relevant and appropriate skills are in short supply, retraining and/or recruitment of new staff will be necessary. Consultation with all stakeholders is essential
- customers must be recognised to the extent that the relationship between them and the in-house team must be taken seriously and managed professionally. Performance monitoring will apply equally to in-house and contracted-out services
- a process of continuous improvement should be implemented to ensure that productivity and standards of quality and performance are raised.

Guidance

Definition of Services

6.4   For contracted-out services, it is generally recognised that success is dependent upon the services, including their interfaces, being clearly defined. This is also true in the case of in-house service provision, but for different reasons. Where services have been contracted out, definition is required to ensure that all necessary services are provided and that no gaps exist between the interfaces of each service. In-house providers require clear definition in order to manage their resources effectively.

6.5   Without clear delineation of roles and responsibilities, it can be difficult to measure performance of in-house staff. Equally, if the customer is unclear as to who is providing what service, it is hard for that provider to both demonstrate and achieve value for money. This is also important in the context of avoiding conflicts of interest because of unclear splits between procurement staff and in-house service staff at the time of preparing tender documents and during the subsequent tendering period.

Identifying Stakeholders

6.6   Stakeholders in the provision of services must be identified, just as they are for contracted-out services. It is important for the in-house team to understand the relative influence of the respective stakeholders as they will potentially be serving many masters simultaneously.

6.7   To ensure the success of the process, each stakeholder's specific requirements must be understood. Whilst it may not always be possible, given the constraints that may be imposed on the in-house team to satisfy all specific requirements, they can be ranked according to their business benefit. In this way, the optimal mix can be established.

In-house Capabilities and Skills

6.8   The in-house service team must be able to adapt to meet changes in requirements in order to support the core business effectively and provide value for money. The ease with which this occurs will clearly depend upon the skills and capabilities of staff and their willingness to continue in training and development. If necessary, in-house teams may have to recruit new staff with the necessary skills.

6.9   In technical areas such as maintenance, many external service providers invest heavily in training to ensure that their staff are competent. This is especially pertinent where new legislation and standards come into force and where it is necessary to retain membership of an industry body or association. To a small in-house team, this may represent a significant time and cost overhead. However, if the in-house team is to satisfy the college's needs these investments must be made.

Departments and Students as Customers

6.10   The in-house service team probably has the benefit of many years' experience of the college, which must not be lost by failing to be responsive to the needs of the customer. Internal departments, their staff and students, must be regarded as the customers and their needs served accordingly. Furthermore, there should be no difference in their attitude towards internal or external customers where the latter could be, for instance, members of the public who are entitled to make some use of the college's facilities. A professional approach can and must be adopted and maintained towards all customers. Many organisations have grasped this issue and it has enabled them to provide a focused service that is also responsive.

In-house Team Approach

6.11   It is essential that the in-house team recognise that they should operate in the same way as would an external service provider and that they will be judged on a similar basis. Given that the college's management will be looking periodically at the market for external service provision, it makes sense for the in-house team to operate in a business-like way so that it can compete fairly when the need arises.

6.12   The in-house team should be examined for its efficiency and effectiveness. The staff that constitute the in-house team must operate as a team if they are to deliver a value-added service. The starting point for engendering team spirit is through sharing common goals and objectives. Government has promoted the establishment of customer charters which set out the type and level of services that can be expected in a number of service industries. This kind of service level agreement (SLA) has the added benefit of articulating the objectives to be achieved by the team. By sharing common goals and key objectives and working as a team, additional benefits can result. This will help the in-house team measure up to the college's expectations, as well as their own.

Service Provision Reviewed and Improved

6.13   The in-house service provider must be proactive in looking for areas to which value can be added. It should not regard service levels as cast in tablets of stone, but as providing the basis for refinement. Their expertise as providers can help to assess whether the perceived service levels are, in fact, the most appropriate. This is particularly relevant in the case of response times when ordering work. If informed discussion can take place as to real needs as opposed to perceived needs, the service, with its corresponding resource levels, can be designed to meet that need. This added-value activity can enable the in-house team to differentiate itself from contracted-out competitors, and intimate knowledge of the college can be used to good effect. That said, knowledge of the college can be no substitute for a service which does not deliver against the customers' needs and overall expectations.

6.14   Many support service processes are labour intensive and are made up of a high volume of low-value activities. Information technology could therefore be of help to the in-house service provider by improving communication and producing appropriate management information. Through the use of low-cost IT, in-house service providers can measure how they are performing against the service level agreed with each identified customer type or group. Thereafter, by means of continuous improvement, increases in performance can be compared and reported against the benchmark (see chapter 12).

Conclusions

6.15   Many of the stages and issues that an in-house team should consider are also relevant in the case of services that are contracted out. The difference lies in the clarity of roles and responsibilities that are usually more obvious in the latter by virtue of the procurement process that has been followed before awarding the contract. The in-house team should try to reach the same position for the benefit of both its customers and its own management needs. This, in turn, will allow more ready measurement of performance and the demonstration of value for money.

CHECKLIST

This checklist is intended to assist with the review and action planning processes.

		Yes	No	Action needed
a.	Have stakeholders in the provision of services been identified and consulted?	☐	☐	☐
b.	Are the services to be provided in house properly defined?	☐	☐	☐
c.	Are the roles and responsibilities of those providing them properly identified?	☐	☐	☐
d.	Has the college clearly assessed and identified current in-house capabilities and skills and augmented those that might be lacking?	☐	☐	☐
e.	Have the roles of departments and students as customers been considered?	☐	☐	☐
f.	Are proper arrangements in place for the review and improvement of service provision?	☐	☐	☐

Chapter 7

Service Specifications, Service Level Agreements and Performance Monitoring

Introduction

7.1   This chapter reviews the need for service specifications and service level agreements (SLAs) arising from the requirements of stakeholders. It identifies the purpose of each and the ways in which they are expected to contribute to the effective management of services provision. Service specifications and SLAs are essential tools in facilities management irrespective of whether services are contracted out or retained in house. Performance monitoring and quality assurance complete the chapter.

Policy Considerations

7.2   The following key issues should be taken into consideration.

- stakeholders must be involved from the outset in specifying the kind of services required and the level of performance that will be acceptable to them, both from in-house and external services providers

- service specifications and SLAs are tools for managing the quality, performance and value of services procured

- a service specification is a document that quantifies the minimum service levels that are acceptable if the customer's requirements are to be met. It provides a benchmark against which the level of services delivered to the customer can be assessed

- an SLA is a commitment by the service provider (in house or contracted out) to the customer to deliver an agreed level of service. It should specify rewards and penalties, yet retain flexibility so that the customer's requirements can be taken into account should circumstances change

- service providers should be involved in the process of updating and improving SLAs and service specifications in order to draw upon their experience of actually providing the service

- performance monitoring of service providers involves reconciling the level of the service delivered to the customer against agreed standards and targets set out in the service specifications and SLAs. Procedures for correcting any discrepancies between these levels requires the participation of both the service provider and the college

- if internal quality targets are to be met, quality of service criteria need to be incorporated into contracts with all service providers. Contracts should stipulate that payments will depend on the performance of the provider in reaching these targets

- colleges may find it useful to describe their performance requirements in terms of factors that are critical to successful service provision. Key performance indicators can be used to measure deviations from specifications and SLAs.

Guidance

Stakeholders' Interests

7.3   Identified stakeholders should be involved in specifying their requirements and the level of performance that will be acceptable. This means:

- involving stakeholders, as far as practicable, in identifying their requirements (for example, through the use of questionnaire surveys and in contributing to the drafting of service specifications and SLAs)

- controlling stakeholder input and changes once the specification has been agreed

- prioritisation by stakeholders of their requirements.

7.4   Colleges may find that they are defining and specifying their requirements for the first time. In such cases, there is a risk that they might unknowingly specify a higher level of service than was received in the past and that, consequently, tenders may be higher than forecast. Colleges can address the risk of such overspecification through the use of value management. This will help guard against overspecification, yet allow standards to be raised over time. Value management is a technique for ensuring that real needs are addressed. Guidance on the technique is given in CUP *Guidance Note 54, Value Management*.

Need for Service Specifications and SLAs

7.5   Service specifications and SLAs are formal documents that should set out:

- the customer's expectations of the quality, performance and value of the services to be provided in a clear and unequivocal manner

- minimum acceptable standards of the service and the customer's requirements that have to be met

- output or performance-oriented measures, concentrating on *what* is to be provided as opposed to *how*

- the agreement between the service provider and the customer for providing a range and target level of services.

7.6   In practice, SLAs are often made by parties within an internal market, that is, between the departments or other operational units within a college and act as a type of contract. This type of contract is not necessarily accompanied by a charge for the service. SLAs are also suitable for situations in which services are contracted out. Here, the SLA supplements the contractual arrangements and is the starting point in developing a partnership agreement.

What is a Service Specification?

7.7   A service specification is a document that quantifies the minimum acceptable (technical) standard of service required by the customer and will generally form a part of the contract with the service provider. The production of the service specification is a prerequisite in the negotiation and drafting of SLAs. They should set out:

- internal standards, relating to corporate or department policy as well as those that have been adopted on previous contracts

- external standards, covering conformance to statutory requirements, British Standards, health and safety legislation, industry standards and manufacturers' recommendations

- procedures the service provider has to comply with in order to achieve the required technical standards

- quality and performance targets.

7.8   The extent of detail in the specification will depend on the importance and complexity of the service or asset item.

What does a service specification contain?

7.9   Table 7 shows the typical format of a service specification. Further guidance on the contents of a service specification is to be found in CUP *Guidance Note 30, Specification Writing* and in chapter 3 of *Procurement* (FEFC/NAO 1997).

Table 7. Contents of a service specification

Section	Contents
Part 1. Terminology	1.1 Definition of terms used
Part 2. Areas/items/services	2.1 Scope of areas/items/services covered by specification
Part 3. External standards	3.1 Statutory requirements 3.2 Manufacturers' recommendations 3.3 Industry-accepted good practice
Part 4. Internal standards	4.1 Corporate/department requirements 4.2 Previously accepted standards
Part 5. Categorisation of areas/items/services	5.1 Detailed procedures for each category 5.2 Frequency of procedures for each category

7.10   In the case of a cleaning contract, for example, the specification could describe the standard of cleanliness to be achieved in terms of the minimum amount of dust or debris which is permitted to remain following cleaning. Another example is in specifying that grass shall be kept below a certain height.

7.11   Annex H contains an example of an extract from a service specification for cleaning showing firstly, concrete specifications and secondly, performance requirements.

Be wary of writing inflexible, over-prescriptive specifications that concentrate on procedures. A good specification focuses on the output, not the procedures that lead to the output.

A prescription for failure

CASE STUDY

The timing of inspections and maintenance of items at a cargo-handling facility was rigidly set out in a programme in the maintenance contract. On a number of occasions, the contractor was unable to carry out the work on the dates specified as it would have seriously disrupted the operation of the facility. The programme was developed without taking into account the need for certain items to be kept operational under very busy conditions. A programme that was more flexible in its timing would have ensured simply that the required number of inspections each year were carried out and the equipment at the facility adequately maintained.

What is an SLA?

7.12   A service level agreement (SLA) is a statement of intention existing between the service provider and the customer — the recipient of the service — setting out a specified level of service. The agreement is formalised by producing a document that describes the following:

- name of each party

- roles and responsibilities of each party

- scope of services that are to be provided

- quality and performance-related targets

- time-related targets

- prices and rates

- resources required

- customer service provider method of communication and interaction

- change procedures.

7.13   The SLA may be of a general format, applicable to a number of services or facilities or it may be customer-, facility- or service-specific. In any event, it will incorporate relevant service specifications.

Development of SLAs

7.14   The customer has certain expectations about the level of service that the service provider should deliver. These expectations need to be translated into formal requirements and targets. In the development of these targets, the service provider should be involved and the agreements developed jointly, so that targets are both appropriate and practicable. An example of a target is where the response to a problem — for instance the failure of a light-fitting or photocopier breakdown — is within a specified period. Stakeholders need to specify what their tolerance threshold is for rectifying a range of failures or malfunctions.

What does an SLA contain?

7.15   The SLA can contain details and targets relating to all or some of the items listed earlier. In principle, the document should identify those measures that the customer will use to judge the level of service he or she receives from the service provider. These measures will generally fall under the following aspects of the service: quality, performance, delivery time, charges for services and the nature of the interaction with the service provider. The SLA can also set out the procedure for incorporating any changes that occur in these targets. Table 8 gives the contents of an SLA.

Table 8. Contents of an SLA based on a total FM service

Section	Contents
Part 1. Agreement details	1.1 Name of parties to the agreement 1.2 Date agreement signed 1.3 Effective date of agreement 1.4 Period of agreement
Part 2. Scope of services — the service specification	2.1 Management of maintenance of buildings, plant and equipment, external landscaping 2.2 Management of minor building works 2.3 Management of accommodation services 2.4 Management of utilities and telecommunications
Part 3. Delivery times, fees	3.1 Service priority categories and times 3.2 Fees and payment
Part 4. Performance	4.1 Submission of performance reports 4.2 Performance measures
Part 5. Customer-service–provider interface	5.1 Communication 5.2 Incentives and penalties 5.3 Customer's rating and feedback 5.3 Procedures for revising SLA

7.16   Further and more detailed guidance on SLAs is given in CUP *Guidance Note 44, Service Level Agreements*. Typical sections of an SLA, taken from CUP's guidance, are reproduced in annex G. Example contents of an SLA are given in annex I. This illustrates the kind of requirements which might be drafted to deal with the submission of performance reports and the measurement of performance.

Critical Success Factors and Key Performance Indicators

7.17   In determining the criteria for measuring the performance (or fulfillment) of an SLA, colleges should consider those factors that are critical to success. Critical success factors (CSFs) are those actions which must be performed well in order for the goals or objectives established by a college to be met satisfactorily. Within each CSF will be one or more key performance indicators (KPIs). These enable a college's senior management to understand, measure and control progress in each of the CSFs. For example, a college may have set a goal of providing the highest-quality service which ensures that each customer receives best value for money. A CSF in achieving that goal would be agreed SLAs. Here, a KPI might be published SLAs to show clearly what has to be achieved and then, subsequently, to say what has been achieved.

7.18   In another example, an internal perspective on productivity, a CSF, would lead to KPIs that highlighted abortive work, backlog and ability (or inability) to perform tasks concurrently. Measures of productivity would include:

- percentage of total work completed at a given time

- percentage of activities planned against unplanned

- percentage of total hours by customer type

- breakdowns against planned preventive maintenance hours.

7.19 Where customer perspectives are concerned, a CSF could be quality for which one of the KPIs would be complaints (or the lack of them) which, in turn, would equate to a measure of the number of complaints over time or, alternatively, a satisfaction rating.

7.20 There are many CSFs and KPIs which interact and combine to bring about a culture and methods which aim to achieve good practice. Performing at the top end of these measures would bring a college to the point of achieving best practice and, with that, best value for money in the management of its services and facilities.

Performance Monitoring

7.21 The customer's view of the quality of a service or product is based on tangible and intangible factors, both of which are important. Tangible factors are those which can be objectively measured, such as the time taken to deliver an item, the charge made and the level of operational performance. Intangible factors include those which are more subjective in nature and, therefore, more difficult to measure; for example, the utility of the item to the customer, its adaptability and advantages over other types or merely the courtesy of the service provider's employees. Factors that are difficult to quantify should not deter their measurement as they can be as important as those that are easily measured. Colleges should, however, be cautioned against imposing too many or overly demanding performance measurements and monitoring of service providers as this risks becoming counter-productive. A sensible approach is to concentrate on the key performance indicators. Table 9 suggests performance measures that could be used, and table 10 a possible scoring system.

Monitoring the times, costs and other performance data for a large number of low-value activities can be time-consuming and counter-productive, unless IT is used.

IT helps to spread the workload

CASE STUDY

The college had decided that, as part of its performance monitoring of the in-house services team, records should be kept of each and every activity performed. The initial reaction from the in-house team manager was that he and his people would probably spend as much time filling in forms as doing the jobs, perhaps even more. It was suggested he make use of a computer, but that did not seem to be the answer he was looking for. In the

Table 9. Example performance measures for planned and unplanned maintenance

Element	Service	Output/measure	Perspective	Comments
1	Planned maintenance performance	Tasks planned in period Tasks completed in period Time taken per task Mean time taken per task Resource attendance in period Number of tasks reworked Percentage of tasks reworked of total tasks in period Service partner resource utilised	by customer by building/location by building/space type by service partner by asset type by asset	resource attendance should enable a snapshot of resource on site at any time undertaking PPM to be considered and reviewed against planned
2	Unplanned maintenance performance	Number of breakdown/faults in period Percentage response times met Number of breakdown/faults completed in period Number of breakdown/faults outstanding in period Time taken per breakdown Mean time taken per breakdown Number of tasks reworked Percentage tasks reworked of total tasks in period	by customer by building/location by building/space type by service partner by asset type by asset	
		Asset availability in period Downtime in period Unplanned stoppages in period Service partner resource utilised	by customer by building/location by building/space type by service partner by asset type	

event, he was persuaded to use a PC with a spreadsheet as part of a popular office automation suite. After some initial instruction, he set up a template on the spreadsheet that provided him with paper forms for recording data which he then keyed in at the end of the day. After some weeks, he began experimenting with the spreadsheet's 'wizard' function to help generate some useful graphs. These were used subsequently to present the college's senior management with the information they had been wanting for some time. Even so, the in-house team manager felt that he was still spending too much time in logging information and then transferring it to the PC. Usually, he had to allocate around one hour at the end of each day. After making enquiries at a local computer store, he acquired a hand-held data capture device which came complete with software and an interface to the PC. Within the week, he had automated the data capture routine and reduced the entire daily ritual to fewer than 10 minutes a day. In fact, on some days, he confessed to not even noticing how long he had spent on that task.

7.22 In practice, the overall performance of a service provider can be determined by monitoring adherence to standards and targets under the following headings:

- conformance to regulations and standards
- quality- and performance-related targets for service delivery
- expenditure targets (see figure 5 on p.92)
- time-related targets
- customer–service provider interaction.

7.23 Performance data can be collected in a number of ways. For example, the service provider may complete worksheets and job reports or feedback from customers might be sought actively in the form of comments on worksheets, complaints and customer surveys.

7.24 Once the college has collected these data they should be used to complete a score-sheet, similar to that presented in table 10, at regular intervals. This should be undertaken for a sample of the services delivered by each service provider based on KPIs. These KPIs will be given in the SLA and contract and will provide a basis for measuring performance in a way that involves both the service provider and the customer.

7.25 On the score-sheet in table 10, column 4 (actual level of service) contains the service provider's measurement of the service or product, based on data and information held by the service provider's organisation. These measures will relate to response times to fault reports, customer surveys, charges made for services and measures of quality levels.

7.26 Customer satisfaction relates to the customer's view of the level of service delivered, based on records held by the college. Reasons for any discrepancies between the three values shown in table 10 then need to be established and corrective action initiated, as necessary. This will entail the active involvement of the college and service provider.

Table 10. Example of unplanned maintenance service

1. Service criteria +	2. Agreed target level of service (targets in SLA or specification)	3. Value +	4. Actual level of service delivered	5. Value	6. Customer satisfaction	7. Value
Regulations/ standards	Work carried out according to health and safety regulations using British Standard products	10	Work carried out according to health and safety regulations using British Standard products	10	Satisfied	10
Performance/ quality	Fault to be rectified such that it is prevented from reoccurring. Minimise level of disruption to users	20	Fault diagnosed and problem rectified. Minor disruption to building users	18	Concern over disruption to work	12
Delivery time	*Minor Lighting Fault* Max response time = 2 hours Max service time = 4 hours *(Total delivery time = 6 hours)*	10	Response time = 3 hours Service time = 2 hours *(Total delivery time = 5 hours)*	8	Concern over delay in response	5
Delivery expenditure	*Minor Lighting Fault* Total cost = £120.00 to £250.00 (range)	10	Total cost = £200.00	10	Satisfied	10
Customer service provider interaction	Keep customer informed of status of work and likely completion time	20	Customer informed that fault had been rectified following completion of work	16	No contact between report of fault and completion	14
Overall service delivery	Work to be carried out according to the targets given above	70	Work carried out satisfactorily, within agreed cost, however, not within agreed response time	62	Work and cost satisfactory, delivery time and contact unsatisfactory	51

Note: + Each activity is assigned a weighted agreed target level of service value. Actual level of service delivered and customer satisfaction values are determined relative to this base value
Report of faulty lighting on section of floor of main building. Date 25/9/96

7.27   The service provider's level of service delivery to the customer will be, to a greater or lesser extent, affected by the quality system that the college has in place. The satisfactory performance of the service provider will be more assured if the quality system is geared to the levels of service performance established in the SLAs. In other words, the ways in which quality and service performance are measured, in accordance with the SLAs, should reflect those prescribed in the college's quality system.

Guard against the absence of, or poor systems for, providing incentives for improved performance. Performance-related systems that aim to raise the standard of service delivery should be based on a fair distribution of rewards and penalties.

Fair or foul play?

CASE STUDY

A college intended to introduce a performance measurement system in its contract with a cleaning contractor as a means of improving the level of service it received. During early discussions with the service provider, the college proposed that incentives in the form of bonus payments were awarded for improved performance and penalties imposed for substandard performance. However, in later discussions, the college revised the system so that good performance was recognised, though not accompanied by financial rewards, whilst financial penalties for poor performance were retained. At that point the cleaning contractor withdrew from the discussions, claiming that there was no real incentive for workers to improve their performance beyond the minimum specified.

Updating Service Specifications and SLAs

7.28   Service specifications should not be regarded as fixed statements of service requirements, but a basis for continuous improvement as circumstances and customers' requirements change. Experience will reveal how better results and improved value for money can be achieved by a change in specification. Service providers should be involved in the process of updating and improving service specifications and SLAs in order to draw upon their experience of actually providing the service. If necessary, visits to other facilities might be necessary to provide insights into how improvements might be possible.

7.29   These actions will ensure that the college is able to determine if the specified service was obtained and so draw lessons for the future. At all times, it is essential that the requirements set out in the service specifications and SLAs should be reflected in the contract with service providers.

Quality Assurance Systems

7.30   If colleges are to receive a satisfactory level of service, not only should they have good quality assurance (QA) systems in place, but their service providers should also. Service providers' QA systems should form an integral part of their service provision. To add value, service providers have to adopt QA to enhance service provision through a reduction in errors and rework. Thus, a quality approach can save money. Colleges should, therefore, include an assessment of tenderers' QA systems as one of their criteria for assessing tenders.

7.31   QA systems generally consist of a policy statement, a quality manual and a work practice manual. The policy statement is the organisation's explicit commitment to a quality-assured system covering its services. The quality manual provides a detailed interpretation of the way in which each of the quality standards are to be met within the context of the operations of the business. The work practice manual explains the detailed procedures that must be followed in order to comply with the QA system. For a QA system to be effective, it needs to be applied as work is being done. Thus, for example, logs and reviews should not be completed retrospectively.

7.32   Contract documents should incorporate quality of service criteria and stipulate that payments will depend on the provider meeting these criteria. These contractual provisions should ensure the quality of services or products of service providers. The issue of penalties and incentives relating to performance standards should be considered following performance reviews.

Conclusions

7.33   Service specifications are an integral part of the process and work alongside SLAs to define the quality and/or performance required when providing a service. Both they and SLAs are fundamental to the business of effective facilities management, irrespective of whether or not the service is contracted out or retained in house. Time spent in preparing tightly written service specifications and SLAs will be amply repaid in the future since such contracts are easier to manage and less prone to misinterpretation. QA systems should be adopted by colleges as a necessary part of facilities management and used to support the work of managers and service providers alike. This ensures, as an absolute minimum, that a consistent set of standards is applied as a basis for seeking continuous improvement.

CHECKLIST

This checklist is intended to assist with the review and action planning processes.

		Yes	No	Action needed
a.	Have identified stakeholders been involved in specifying their requirements as to the level of performance that will be acceptable?	☐	☐	☐
b.	Have service specifications and service level agreements been prepared?	☐	☐	☐
c.	Have the critical success factors and key performance indicators for the provision of services been identified?	☐	☐	☐
d.	Are proper performance arrangements for performance monitoring of the provision of service in place?	☐	☐	☐
e.	Does the facilities management strategy provide for the updating of service specifications and service level agreements?	☐	☐	☐
f.	Does the college have quality assurance systems in place?	☐	☐	☐

Chapter 8

Legal, and Health and Safety Considerations

Introduction

8.1   This chapter offers guidance to help colleges ensure they provide a safe and healthy place of work for staff and customers. It reviews the legislation and describes the characteristics of a well-managed health and safety regime. Checklists are included to indicate the scope of matters for which attention is required. Whilst every care has been exercised in identifying relevant legislation, it should not be regarded as a complete guide to health and safety legislation. It is essential that colleges verify the extent to which legislation might apply to them.

Policy Considerations

8.2   The following key issues should be taken into consideration.

- compliance with health and safety legislation applies to everybody in the workplace. It applies to colleges, including shared parts of buildings and the grounds in which the college is set

- a competent person must be appointed to the college's staff or as a consultant to assist in implementing and complying with health and safety legislation, whether services are retained in house or contracted out

- a general health and safety policy statement must be produced by the college and this must be communicated to all stakeholders. An organisation and administration management method for implementing the policy must be produced and its effectiveness measured

- policies, detailed safety rules and safe working practices to ensure compliance with health and safety legislation must be devised and implemented and regularly reviewed.

Guidance

Relevant Legislation

8.3   The principal legislation is that contained in the *Health and Safety at Work Act 1974*. Where colleges have industrial workshops, additional legislation applies, for instance the *Noise at Work Regulations 1989*. Where building works are carried out on the premises, the *Construction, Design and Management (CDM) Regulations 1994* will also apply. Current legislation will be progressively tightened, and *CDM* is just the beginning of a major push at reducing accidents and the hazards that lead to them. Colleges must recognise that safety management will become a significant item on the agenda for operating a facility of any description.

General Policy

8.4   Colleges must have a general policy on health and safety. The requirements of this general policy are:

- to provide and maintain, as far as is practicable, a healthy and safe place of work

- to take responsibility for compliance with relevant legislation including:

    – *Construction (Health, Safety and Welfare) Regulations 1996*

    – *Construction, Design and Management (CDM) Regulations 1994*

    – *Health and Safety at Work Act 1974*

    – *Workplace (Health, Safety and Welfare) Regulations 1992*

    – *Management of Health and Safety at Work Regulations 1992*

    – *Provision and Use of Work Equipment Regulations 1992*

    – *Personal Protective Equipment at Work Regulations 1992*

    – *Manual Handling Operations Regulations 1992*

    – *Reporting of Injuries, Diseases and Dangerous Occurrences Regulations 1995*

    – *Control of Substances Hazardous to Health Regulations 1988* (amended 1994, 1996 and 1997)

    – *Electricity at Work Regulations 1989*

    – *Health and Safety (Safety Signs and Signals) Regulations 1996*

    – *Health and Safety (Display Screen Equipment) Regulations 1992*

    – *Health and Safety (First Aid) Regulations 1981*

    – *Disability Discrimination Act 1995*

    – *Fire Precautions Act 1971*

    – *Noise at Work Regulations 1989.*

8.5   Colleges need to be aware that their responsibilities for health and safety extend beyond college staff and students to the extent that no activity should pose risks to visitors or persons outside the premises. The college has responsibility for anybody and anyone who is affected by the action of an employee and the college's policy statement and risk assessments must reflect this. It is necessary to appoint a person who can be judged to be competent in implementing and ensuring that the college complies with health and safety legislation. Employers must have access to a 'competent person' (who could be an employee or contractor consultant) and must ensure that he or she has adequate training time and resources to discharge his or her duties under health and safety legislation.

Organisation and Administration

8.6   In all cases, it is necessary to identify responsibilities as imposed by legislation at all levels of management and supervision and not just for those staff who are directly involved in the day-to-day management of facilities; for example, members of the governing body and the procurement officer will have roles to play.

8.7   Care should be taken to apportion responsibility in line with authority, with resources to cover the administration procedures for dealing with accidents and contingency plans for handling power cuts, bomb alerts, flood and fire. Student safety representatives and/or committees should always be involved.

8.8   Proper consideration should be given to providing information about substances, plant and machinery to employees and to updating this information. Additionally, training in health and safety responsibilities for all employees should be provided.

Safety Rules and Practice

8.9   Colleges will need to assess the risks to the health and safety of employees and anyone else affected by the activities of the college (for example, staff, customers, visitors and the general public) and devise means of implementing preventive and protective measures. Assessment must cover planning, organisation, control, monitoring and reviews. There is a close link between risk assessment and arrangements specified in the policy statement.

Ongoing Management

8.10   With a policy and a management system in place, colleges must monitor and review arrangements to achieve progressive improvement in health and safety. Improvement will be enhanced through the development of policies, approaches to implementation and techniques of risk control.

8.11   Colleges must take account of the special problems faced by disabled persons and others with special needs and should ensure that appropriate measures are taken to ensure their health and safety. This may involve adaptation of existing means of access to and escape from buildings. Colleges should seek professional advice on how their buildings and other facilities comply with relevant legislation, including the *Disability Discrimination Act 1995*, as well as making themselves aware of the expectations of staff and students, especially those with special needs.

8.12   The following checklists will enable colleges to monitor their adherence to, and progress against, health and safety legislation.

Organisation

- are policy, management and organisation, safety rules and procedures in place?

- are these details available to all staff and customers?

- have arrangements been made for consultation with staff and student bodies?

Noticeboards

- is the safety policy clearly displayed?

- is the health and safety law poster displayed?

- is a copy of the Employer's Liability insurance certificate displayed?

- are the names of trained first-aiders displayed?

- are emergency procedures displayed?

Accident reporting

- is an accident book held on the premises?

- are staff and students aware of the location of the accident book?

- are internal accident report forms held?

- is the Health and Safety Executive (HSE) leaflet, *Everyone's Guide to RIDDOR*, available?

Training

- have all people with health and safety functions received specific health and safety training?

- have all staff attended a general health and safety awareness course?

- are records maintained of training undertaken?

- have staff received appropriate specialist training, for example NEBOSH national general certificate in occupational safety and health?

First aid

- is a current list of first-aiders and their locations displayed on each noticeboard?

- how many first-aiders are there and how are they spread throughout the buildings?

- does each first-aider have an adequate first-aid box?

- who keeps top-up supplies for first-aid boxes?

- who is responsible for inspecting all first-aid boxes for their contents, visibility and availability?

- who organises first-aid training?

- which organisation supplies first-aid training?

- are records of first-aid training adequate and up to date?

- are treatment record sheets available by each first-aid box or located with the accident book?

Fire precautions

- is there a fire certificate for the buildings?

- who has delegated responsibility for fire precautions?

- how often are evacuation drills carried out?

- are full records of these drills kept, including building clearance times?

- how often are fire alarms tested and are full records of these tests maintained?

- how often are smoke and heat detectors tested?

- is this in accordance with manufacturers' recommendations or fire certificate?

- are full records of these tests maintained?

- how often are fixed hose-reel and sprinkler systems (if applicable) tested?

- are full records of these tests maintained?

- do the drills and tests comply with the conditions of the fire certificate?

- are records kept of visits by the fire officer?

- is there a service contract for the maintenance of fire extinguishers and other fire control equipment?

- are there adequate fire extinguishers of the correct type?

- is there at least one fire warden for each floor?

- what training, practice or regular meetings are arranged for fire wardens?

- how often are the offices inspected in relation to fire precautions?

- is there a procedure for notifying the fire authority of alterations to buildings?

Statutory risk assessments

- have assessments been carried out for all display screen equipment workstations?

- is there a valid risk assessment for the premises?

- have all hazardous substances been assessed under the *Control of Substances Hazardous to Health Regulations 1988? (COSHH)*

- have any other assessments been carried out, for example lifting of loads and personal protective equipment?

- are the control measures specified in the risk assessments being adhered to?

Inspections and audits

- how often does the facilities manager or other person with delegated responsibility inspect the offices for physical hazards?

- when was the last inspection carried out?

- when was the last audit of procedures carried out and by whom?

Work equipment

- who is responsible for arranging annual lift inspections, where applicable?

- are the premise's electrical installation and all portable electrical appliances and equipment tested by a competent person, as required by the *Electricity at Work Regulations 1989*, with the results of those tests and any necessary remedial action properly recorded?

- are there procedures for inspecting and maintaining all work equipment?

- is the use of potentially dangerous work equipment restricted to authorised persons and are those persons properly trained?

Personal protective equipment

- have assessments been carried out to determine the personal protective equipment (PPE) requirements of staff and students?

- have records of these assessments been kept?

- is all necessary PPE available?

- are records kept of PPE issued?

- have staff been trained in the use and maintenance requirements of PPE, if applicable?

- has adequate storage for PPE been provided?

Off campus

- have risks associated with visiting other sites or working outside been assessed?

- is a procedure for lone working defined and in use?

- are staff aware of these procedures and have they been trained in them?

Employing contractors

- are contractors used for window-cleaning, maintenance, electrical installation and so on?

- is a health and safety questionnaire completed by each contractor carrying out work on the premises before they are engaged?

- is there a 'contractors on site' policy document which all contractors must read and then sign as evidence of their awareness of their duties and obligations?

- who vets these questionnaires and on what basis is it decided that a contractor is competent to carry out the work?

- what information is given to contractors on emergency procedures, safety rules and access?

- who is responsible for ensuring compliance with *CDM*?

Notices

- are all necessary compliance and safety signs in place?

Conclusions

8.13   Providing a safe and healthy place of work for staff and customers not only means compliance with statutory requirements, but also safeguards the people working there. Guidance in this important area cannot be exhaustive. Colleges are advised to ensure they comply with the requirements by seeking professional advice.

CHECKLIST

This checklist is intended to assist with the review and action planning processes.

		Yes	No	Action needed
a.	Are the college and its advisers aware of relevant legislation in relation to the management and occupation of premises with particular emphasis on health and safety issues?	☐	☐	☐
b.	Have the college's requirements for implementing health and safety legislation been properly identified and arrangements made for their proper organisation and administration?	☐	☐	☐
c.	Has a proper assessment of the risk to health and safety for staff and anybody else affected by the activities of the college been completed?	☐	☐	☐
d.	Have the means of implementing appropriate measures been devised?	☐	☐	☐
e.	Have responsibilities for health and safety matters been identified and placed?	☐	☐	☐

Chapter 9

Facilities Management Service Providers

Introduction

9.1　In this chapter, the main types of service which are on offer in the market-place are reviewed (see *Thinking About Facilities Management*, The Business Round Table, 1996).　There will be variations to these types according to particular circumstances, but they are, otherwise, the most common.　Colleges should be aware of the state of the market for facilities management.　If necessary, colleges should consult trade associations or potential service contractors to test the market directly, as well as enquire about suitable companies.

Policy Considerations

9.2　The following key issues should be taken into consideration.

- there are three main types of service provision in the market-place: managing agent, managing contractor and total facilities management company.　There are also variations on them.　In all cases, the choice of approach to service provision has to be based on identified needs

- all approaches attract costs for the college in managing and administering contracts.　Colleges need to weigh the risks and costs of the different approaches.　Flexibility of service provision may also be a factor that has to be taken into account

- the employment of a total facilities management company — effectively providing a single point of responsibility — will not relieve the college from managing the contract and interface between the contractor and customers.　There are bound to be costs in connection with the management of even a single appointment.

Guidance

Preliminary Approach

9.3　Colleges will have determined which services to contract out and will have done so by taking account of the market (see chapter 3).　Earlier actions will have established whether or not the market is capable of delivering what is required by the college.　An important consideration for colleges should be the bundling of individual services in a way that will provide best value for money (VFM).　There are two aspects to consider.

First, colleges will have worked out how best to arrange their contracting out to ensure that VFM is likely to be achieved. Second, service providers will take a commercial view on what is profitable for them. Bundling of services can prove to be an attraction for service providers; likewise, carving up the totality of facilities management into very small contracts may not. It is also useful to recognise that arrangements which may involve a lot of subcontracting (and sub-subcontracting) can confer a financial disadvantage because cost is added at each point in the supply chain without necessarily adding value. Preliminary enquiries — in the form of market testing as described in chapter 3 — will, however, help to establish the most advantageous approach to the bundling of services, as well as mitigating against the likelihood of redundancy occurring in the supply chain. This can be achieved by considering various combinations of services for which indicative quotations can then be sought.

9.4   Colleges will also need to consider the attributes of service provision which are of most importance to them so that they are able to identify the most suitable service providers (see chapter 3). Guidance on the qualitative criteria which can be used to help in weighting different attributes of service can also be found in *Estate Management in Further Education Colleges: A Good Practice Guide* (FEFC/NAO 1996). This provides a basis for subsequently judging the suitability of service providers before an invitation to tender and, thereafter, in assessing their tender.

9.5   College representatives should be appraised of the financial standing of any service provider before entering into a contract with them (see chapter 5). Credit references should be sought in addition to performance references from existing clients. Failure of a service provider, large or small, will have implications for the college. Whilst it is never possible to eliminate the likelihood of this happening, its occurrence can be minimised by taking up references with reliable sources.

Types of Service Provision

9.6   There are essentially three main types of service provision. They range from the use of an external organisation or individual who manages the college's own staff, through the appointment of a contractor to manage some or all service providers, to an arrangement where all facilities are managed by an external entity offering a single point of responsibility. Figure 3 shows the three main types in terms of their contractual and management (communication) links.

Figure 3. Three types of contractual arrangement

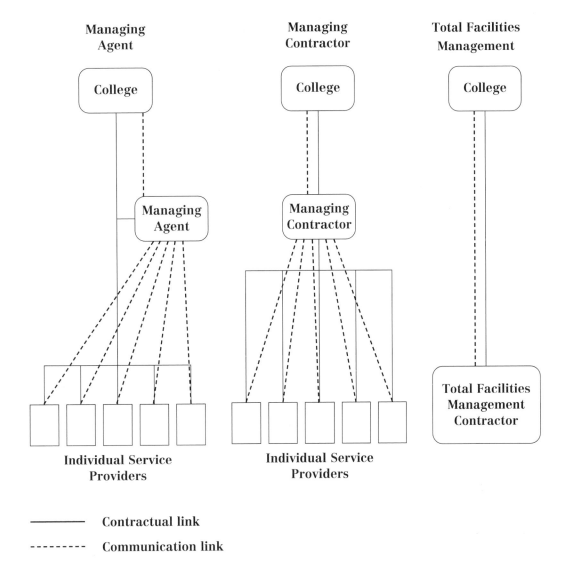

Managing Agent

9.7   This arrangement is adopted when the college has determined that it wishes to retain its own staff, but does not have the skill or expertise with which to manage them efficiently and effectively. By bringing in an external organisation to manage the facilities, the college is essentially appointing a client representative. This person — as invariably the appointment will specify an individual — will act almost as though he or she were part of the permanent establishment of the college. The client representative (managing agent) will perform better and more reliably if performance criteria are laid down, as indeed would an in-house manager. Under this arrangement, contracts with service suppliers will be with the college.

9.8   There are distinct and, perhaps, obvious advantages in adopting this arrangement. Both the agent and the various service contractors can be selected on the basis of competitive tendering. Moreover, the appointment (or re-appointment) of the agent should not affect contracts with service suppliers or vice versa. Dissatisfaction with a given contractor would not place other contracts at risk; indeed, it could positively assist in those cases where poor performance has had a knock-on effect.

9.9   The managing agent approach offers considerable flexibility for the college to find and then hold on to the combination of contracts that suits it best. There is no reason why services should not be part in house and part contracted out. The appointment of a managing agent is especially crucial to success as the college would be using this person to contribute expertise and exercise judgement when deciding between in-house and contracted-out service provision.

9.10   There are potential disadvantages for colleges which adopt this approach. For example, it is possible that gaps might occur between the scope of the various contracts, including that of the managing agent. Managing agents can be made responsible for ensuring that the scope of service contracts is such that gaps do not occur.

9.11   From a risk perspective, the college is probably moderately exposed. It may have to accept the possibility of introducing an uncertain combination of risk factors by its own selection of contractors (including the managing agent) on an individual or piecemeal basis. The reasoning here is that a number of contractors coming together for the first time will place extra demands on the managing agent. Sound relationships between different contractors are needed if services are to be provided properly and facilities are to operate effectively. These relationships may take some time to develop. A conscious effort will, therefore, be required on the part of the managing agent to integrate the work of the different contractors in such a way that they become moulded into one efficient team.

9.12   Colleges may also find that administration costs increase as the number of separate contracts rises. Allowance must be made for this when evaluating contracting out as an option. Risks can be mitigated and administration reduced by appointing the managing agent first and requiring that he or she establishes the suitability of service contractors. Colleges embarking on this route should allocate adequate resources to planning and implementation.

Managing Contractor

9.13   Under this arrangement there is one contract between the college and the appointed contractor. Subcontractors (there are bound to be several) will be under contract to the managing contractor and so will not have a contractual relationship with the college. This means that colleges have a single point of contact with the contractor on all matters pertaining to the service provision. Thus, if a service falls below the required performance for work carried out by a subcontractor, the college need only direct its complaint to the contractor. However, as the chain of command is longer, delays in receiving prompt action may occur. Although the subcontractors are contracted to the managing contractor, the college should protect its position by ensuring they have the right to approve the selection of subcontractors.

9.14   Since under the managing contractor approach there is a single point of contact, there should be a sizeable reduction in paperwork and fewer payments. Gaps in service provision should be eliminated because the managing contractor is required to ensure that they simply do not occur. By using a contractor to undertake some or all of the work, with the support of subcontractors, colleges are able to mitigate much financial risk. Contractors are generally paid a fee and this can, of course, be related to their performance. The college is, despite the limitation of being in just one contract, able to see where its money is being spent because open-book accounting is usually adopted.

9.15   Under open-book accounting, the college has access to all the contractor's premises, books and records, including invoices from subcontractors. This right to access is necessary as the managing contractor may insist on larger trade discounts than normal, or may demand some other preferential terms which are not consistent with good practice. In these cases, the managing contractor's approach may result in poor performance by the subcontractor and, therefore, poor service to the college. Open-book accounting also ensures that there are few misunderstandings on the cost of services.

9.16   On the down side, changes to a contract, once it is formalised, will be more difficult to make than under the managing agent arrangement, unless they are provided for in advance.

Total Facilities Management

9.17   Colleges are able to pass the full responsibility for managing their facilities to a single organisation for a fixed price. This does, however, require the college to provide the contractor with sufficient scope to be able to manage the various services efficiently. Whilst total facilities management might appear to provide an ideal solution, because it provides a one-stop shop for the college, the reality can be that the contractor subcontracts all or most of the work to other organisations. Since there is just one contract — that between the college and the total facilities management contractor — there is the chance that terms and conditions between the contractor and subcontractor do not mirror those of the (main) contract. Difficulties can arise because terms and conditions which are embodied in the contract between the college and the contractor may allow for situations which are not subsequently recognised in the contract with the subcontractor or vice versa.

9.18   The total facilities management contractor may be better able to offer a more complete and competitive solution to a college's needs than in the case of the managing agent or managing contractor. Relationships built up over years between the contractor and (specialist) subcontractors may mean that efficient working relationships are established from the start.   Total facilities management can provide a sound solution for colleges. However, this is possible only if the college is prepared to spend time identifying the right basis for such an arrangement and then in selecting the best contractor.

9.19   In practice, things can go wrong. Reasons include the contractor's relationship with his subcontractors. For example, the total facilities management contractor may insist on larger discounts than normal or some other preferential terms which are not consistent with good practice. Also, during the currency of a contract, the contractor may decide to change subcontractors. These decisions are not always made for reasons of improving performance; they may arise because the contractor is seeking to increase margins through the employment of a cheaper subcontractor. As with any change, newly appointed subcontractors — for whatever reason they are employed — will undergo a learning curve. In this case, colleges should ensure that the procedure for assigning or subcontracting is open to inspection and that they have the right under the contract to prior approval before such assignment or subcontracting. Open-book accounting should also be in place.

9.20   In terms of risk, the college is only moderately exposed and can derive a good deal of comfort from knowing that there is a single point of contact and less administration. Value for money may not be quite as good as in the managing agent case, though against that has to be weighed the additional cost of organising and managing many more individual contracts, under a managing agent approach.

Which Approach is Best?

9.21   The choice of approach for a college would depend on many factors. If, however, the procedures outlined in chapter 3 have been followed, colleges should be able to see which approach is best for them and proceed with confidence.

9.22   Competition in selecting the best option, based on value for money, has to be the criterion applied to all situations. Whether a college chooses to manage all service contracts itself (perhaps through an appointed managing agent) or passes the responsibility to a third party, there will be a cost and risks involved. Colleges must decide which risks they are prepared to take and at what cost, and which risks to pass to someone else for what may well be a higher sum. Flexibility is a factor that has to be taken into account, along with the attendant cost and risk.

9.23   The chosen approach should be one which will provide value for money for the college and its customers. Total facilities management has obvious attractions, but it will not relieve the college from managing the contract and the interface between the contractor and its customers. In deciding between the approaches, colleges must consider carefully how to ensure that customer needs are fully addressed. A VFM solution is not one that compromises on customer satisfaction.

9.24   Finally, colleges must always take into account the track record of any contractor or agent they may be considering, together with an understanding of their particular expertise.

Conclusions

9.25   There are basically three ways of buying services from the market-place. The first involves the employment of a managing agent under contract to the college, acting as the client's representative. The second is the appointment of a managing contractor. This differs from the former in that the contractor takes responsibility for engaging and managing the various services contracts for a fee. The last of these principal ways is where a single point of responsibility is established with one contractor providing all services. The best approach to take will be the one that is most closely aligned to the needs of the college and which delivers best value for money. If the ground is thoroughly prepared beforehand, the choice of option will be obvious. Attention can then turn to the selection of the best contractors.

CHECKLIST

This checklist is intended to assist with the review and action planning processes.

		Yes	No	Action needed
a.	Does the college understand the types of service provision available and in particular the distinctions between the roles of the managing agent, managing contractor and a total facilities management approach?	☐	☐	☐
b.	Has the college followed an appropriate procedure to identify which approach would best suit its current requirements?	☐	☐	☐
c.	Has the college understood where the balance of risks lies for the type of service provision selected?	☐	☐	☐
d.	Has the college taken all the necessary steps to verify the capabilities and financial standing of the service providers it intends to select?	☐	☐	☐

Chapter 10

Managing Service Provider and Supplier Relationships

Introduction

10.1   In this chapter, we discuss how colleges can get the best from their service providers and suppliers. Rather than seeing service providers and suppliers as simply a source which can be tapped as and when required, they can be used to help produce greater economy through less waste and a generally more efficient process. Annex B has more guidance on establishing and maintaining good supplier relationships.

Policy Considerations

10.2   The following key issues should be taken into consideration.

- all service providers and suppliers have to be managed. Buying a service without concern for the ensuing relationship might be to ignore a useful source of skill and expertise

- co-operative relationships with service providers and suppliers can provide greater certainty of provision without being uncompetitive or compromising on quality or performance

- partnering is the most common form of co-operative relationship for managing service providers and suppliers. It is not, however, an answer for all needs and situations. Even so, partnering is an acceptable alternative to competitive tendering provided it too has a competitive element

- relationships imply working towards goals which have to be shared by the college and service provider (or supplier) alike. Continuous improvement is a necessary part of the culture and is one that must include measurable targets in all arrangements including partnering.

Guidance

Who are the Suppliers?

10.3   Suppliers are any organisation from which a service or supply is procured. Usually, they are regarded as someone or somebody who gets paid to provide —

nothing more, nothing less. Where a supplier is responsible for something that can be easily provided by many others, such as cleaning, there may seem little need to bother about developing relationships beyond those of a straightforward commercial arrangement. However, this ignores the possibility that the supplier's knowledge about products and processes could be used to reduce waste and raise productivity. Clearly, where the supplier is of economic significance to the college, it makes sense to explore ways in which unnecessary cost might be eliminated. Having a close working relationship with the supplier can achieve this goal, yet does not necessarily risk being uncompetitive.

10.4   So far, the supplier has been discussed in the familiar sense of someone or somebody that might provide a service such as cleaning, security or day-to-day repairs. The term 'supplier' needs to be broadened to embody any person or organisation external to the college who can contribute to its success or failure. A contract cleaning company is a clear example, but so is a local architect working on a classroom refurbishment programme. Each has a relationship with the college and this has to be managed; otherwise, the relationship is likely to fail at some point.

Types of Relationship

10.5   When considering the nature of the relationship that a college should have with its suppliers, it is important not to focus on contractual arrangements until a sensible basis for working with a supplier has been found. Contractual arrangements should not override how a given product or service should be provided.

10.6   Supplier relationships can be improved by providing incentives for performance which exceeds agreed targets and by making use of the expertise that many suppliers undoubtedly possess. Successful relationships will come from treating suppliers as partners, even where there is a contract based on a traditional price competition.

10.7   Partnering is a practice which has become popular in the property and construction industries. Many see it as the means by which they can avoid bidding competitively for a service: it is not. The aim is to build a business relationship that is founded on trust. It is not a way of working around financial constraints. Partnering aligns the objectives of the customer and supplier in an attempt to maximise the benefits to both (see annex B). For the college, there can be savings from not having to tender repeatedly; for the supplier it can mean regular work from a customer whose requirements are better understood than they would otherwise be. Business arranged in this way can bring about significant savings over the medium to longer term. A comparison of partnering with a traditional arrangements is given in table 11.

Table 11. Partnering compared with a traditional contracting arrangement

Partnering	Traditional contracting
Innovative, not well-developed	Established, well-developed
Ability to negotiate on price	Difficult to negotiate on price
Close interaction between parties	Arm's length relationship
Quality improvement possible	Quality likely to be minimum specified
Proactive contractor response	Reactive contractor response
Disputes less likely	Disputes common
Long-term benefits	Short-term gains

10.8   The essence of partnering is that the customer usually determines to work with a select number of firms or individuals who will share all the work in a prescribed area. This is easy to achieve if you happen to be a regular and large procurer of new buildings. For colleges, the opportunities to partner are more limited, though do exist in the sense of sharing with someone or somebody who will provide a real gain to the college. Partnering could exist in transportation services and vehicle maintenance. Another example is where colleges collaborate on the bulk purchasing of utilities supplies to form a procurement consortium. Such arrangements create an economy of scale which can provide smaller colleges with better value for money than under an arrangement in which they attempt to negotiate on their own. An additional benefit from this kind of collaboration is that expertise and risks are also shared.

A clean sweep

CASE STUDY

It had long been the view that cleaning was a generally predictable activity for which there was an accepted approach. This tended to mean that the contractor's supervisor would requisition supplies of cleaning agents and other consumables as and when required from a local supplier. On the operations front, there was a daily pattern which, though not perfect, was accepted as the way things were done. For some time, the facilities manager had been wondering how she could reduce what appeared to be a wasteful and, therefore, expensive approach. The time was fast approaching when the college was due to test the market for a range of services, including cleaning. The facilities manager took the initiative to talk to a couple of local service providers who were working on various office developments on the nearby science park. After a short time, it became apparent that the college was probably paying far too much for cleaning. The reasons were that it was buying in expensive and perhaps unnecessary agents and consumables and that the frequency and timing of a large amount of cleaning was unnecessary. In the event, the facilities manager asked all three service providers to consider tendering for the cleaning contract on the basis that the

successful contractor would be asked to enter into a partnering arrangement. Whilst a contract would still be in place, there would be flexibility to explore ways of improving quality and performance and reducing cost. Two of the three accepted the invitation, illustrating how a partnering arrangement can allow colleges to benefit from the expertise of service providers to everyone's benefit.

10.9 In the study of current practice, the most common form of partnering was in the supply of energy. Consultants had been engaged by many colleges to advise on the most cost-effective source of supply. Since tariffs change regularly, it is not always possible for those who go to the market infrequently (such as annually) to keep abreast of changes. Some colleges seem also to rely upon consultants to advise them on their energy use. However, a well-managed college should be able to do this for itself. By capturing details of consumption on a computer-based spreadsheet a college can then test the implications of the various tariffs offered by different suppliers. Using simple sensitivity analysis — the classic 'what if'? — colleges could see what the risk of adopting a particular supplier might be, given a change in circumstances. Additionally, colleges should benchmark their spending and consumption against other colleges or similar bodies.

What Kind of Relationship is Needed?

10.10 Few services or supplies are of exactly the same degree of importance. For colleges, failure in certain of them could prove disastrous (for instance a failure to test electrical appliances) whilst other types of failure might be tolerated or at least a means found to minimise their impact. It is therefore important for colleges to recognise where the kinds of suppliers with whom they are dealing lie within the matrix shown in table 12. Locating suppliers in the correct position within the matrix focuses attention on the kind of relationship that has to be managed (Gadde 1996). Procedures will then need to reflect the different emphases that are required of the relationship. In this way, it should be possible for colleges to achieve higher levels of service from suppliers.

Table 12. Locating service providers and suppliers according to their relationship

| | | Economic significance of service provider/supplier | |
		Major	Minor
Degree of integration	Close	Cleaning, security	Helpdesk
	Loose	Electricity, gas	Condition survey

10.11 Understanding the kinds of relationship that are possible is only the beginning. Colleges will need to adopt appropriate controls and incentives which may well differ between sets of relationships. It should be possible for colleges to devise relationships with individual suppliers which are more closely aligned with the needs of both parties. For example, the close relationship demanded of a cleaning contract might embody incentives for ensuring that areas are cleaned in ways and at times that provide maximum flexibility for customers. The extent of the requirements might be so complicated that without a close working relationship — perhaps founded as a partnering arrangement — the quality of service expected might be unattainable.

10.12   In another example, that of the helpdesk, a well-managed service for responding to enquiries and complaints could yield worthwhile savings for the college. For instance, helpdesk staff who are well versed in technical procedures and competent in some aspects of problem-solving could obviate the need for further action, by providing advice there and then on how to deal with problems concerning heating, ventilation or other aspects of engineering services. Savings from the avoidance of calling out service operatives could amply repay the cost of providing the helpdesk. However, helpdesk staff would need to be specially trained to do this, for which the college may then have to pay more for their services. Establishing a close working relationship with the service provider — or assessing the capabilities of prospective providers — would seem sensible. In terms of controls, the service provider could be rewarded for reductions in the costs of calling out service engineers and, if the situation arises, penalised for failing to deal promptly and sensibly with enquiries (see chapter 11 for further comment on incentivisation).

10.13   In other areas, for example the supply of a utility such as electricity, there may be little point in attempting to bring about a closer working relationship other than with neighbouring colleges in arranging bulk purchases. More often than not, the greater the involvement or interaction of the college with the supplier, the more indirect costs there will be.

Conclusions

10.14   The relationship with a supplier does not end once the contract has been placed. If anything, that is the beginning. It will take a lot of hard work to manage the relationship successfully into the future. Ways can always be found to add incentives for both sides to ensure the satisfactory performance of a supply or service provision. Setting targets as part of a programme of continuous improvement is possible. By engaging the skill of the supplier in the process — as opposed to more conventional arrangements which actively exclude it — better ways might be found of delivering customer satisfaction at lower cost. Partnering or other forms of co-operative relationship can be entirely appropriate for a college in its search for value for money. However, partnering is not a panacea and its selection must be based on a well-founded case.

CHECKLIST **This checklist is intended to assist with the review and action planning processes.**

		Yes	No	Action needed
a.	Has the college identified its key suppliers?	☐	☐	☐
b.	Does the college understand the economic significance of each of its service providers and suppliers?	☐	☐	☐
c.	Has the college considered instances where partnering, or some other co-operative arrangement, might be preferable to traditional, competitive bidding?	☐	☐	☐
d.	Are appropriate strategies in place for managing the relationship with suppliers?	☐	☐	☐

Chapter 11

Contract Management and Financial Control

Introduction

11.1   This chapter provides guidance on contract management and financial monitoring. These aspects of facilities management can represent a significant resource issue for colleges, not least because they are ongoing commitments.   As such, they will always involve a minimum level of resource whether services are contracted out or retained in house. In these respects, the role of the intelligent client function (see chapter 1 and annex A) is one that should develop over time as working knowledge of how contractors perform is built up. For the purpose of this guidance, contract management and financial monitoring is deemed to include:

- contractual approach and terms

- payments structure

- cost monitoring

- performance monitoring

- change control

- contract administration and review.

Policy Considerations

11.2   The following key issues should be taken into consideration.

- colleges need to develop the informed or intelligent client function (ICF) if they are to manage contracts and control finances. This applies irrespective of whether or not services are contracted out

- service providers should receive reimbursement or penalty appropriate to their performance against the service specification and service level agreement (SLA)

- in-house providers should be assessed against the same criteria as external providers. Any changes that are required should be controlled in accordance with the principles of the original contract

- contract costs should be monitored against both the budget and tender price on a basis that is appropriate to their duration and size

- the level or extent of contract review should be appropriate to the value and complexity of the contract. For most services, this period should be 12 months unless otherwise agreed as part of specific private partnership and investment arrangements (see chapter 14).

Guidance

Contractual Approach and Terms

11.3 In all cases, payment will be dependent upon performance. Contracts should define, therefore, how payments will be adjusted when performance deviates from that which is acceptable. Given that facilities management is about the provision of services, rather than tangible products, it is important to see reimbursement as something that should vary according to the performance of the service provider. This will mean that colleges have to define the level of poor service delivery at which reduced payments are no longer a sufficient redress and the college can terminate the contract. In this connection, contracts may need to contain a clause stating that, if the college does terminate the contract, the service provider can go to arbitration or some other cheaper and quicker form of alternative dispute resolution method.   Annex F describes how contracts should be approached and what terms should apply.

Payments

11.4 Colleges will need to be aware of the implications of cashflow for both themselves and their service providers. Whilst colleges can be expected to have up-to-date financial information and so be appraised of their cashflow position, service providers may not be so well placed. It may prove beneficial, therefore, if service providers were required to submit a cashflow forecast for their service provision before the contract comes into effect and to keep this up to date. In this way, both colleges and service providers will know what their likely pattern of payments will be. This will also help in measuring actual performance against that forecast. Regular payments to service providers are essential to ensuring that they do not fail financially. It is dangerous to assume that where a service provider is large, they will always have funds flowing in from other contracts. The problem can sometimes be that too many clients think the same, resulting in failure.

11.5 The structure and format of payment documentation should be clear and simple; an example is shown in figure 4. The advantage of the format is that as the gross value of services is recalculated each month, any overpayment in a previous month will be automatically taken into account without the need for credit notes. In addition, the value of planned contract services and any changes to them are clearly identified.

Figure 4. Monthly payment form

WESTIN COLLEGE   **Month:** 9

Contract: Mechanical &   **Service Provider:**   **Ref:**
Electrical Maintenance   Emeny (Contractors) Ltd   PPM01

Covering Period: September 1996   **Payment No:** 9

Contract Sum: £449,000.000

Gross Values to Date

- Planned contract services   £   176,000.00

- Changes to planned services   £   22,000.00

- Unplanned/reactive services   £   112,000.00
                                    _____

Sub-Total   £   310,000.00

Less previous   £   236,000.00
                                                               _____

Payment Due   £   74,000.00

VAT @ 17.5%   £   12,950.00
                                                               _____

Total Amount Due   £   86,950.00

Authorised by: **Date:** 1/10/96

_____
Supervising Officer

Figure 5. Cost control report form

WESTIN COLLEGE					Month: 9
(A) Service or Service Element	**(B)** Contract Sum	**(C)** Changes	**(D)** Anticipated final account (B+C)	**(E)** Gross Value of Service To Date	**(F)** Comments
Planned Preventive Maintenance	449,000	22,000	471,000	176,000	PPM programme behind schedule.
Unplanned/ Reactive Services	–	112,000	112,000	112,000	High level of reactive repairs.
Totals	449,000	134,000	583,000	288,000	

Cost Monitoring

11.6   A report should be completed by the college in order to ensure that contract costs are monitored and controlled systematically. An example format is shown in figure 5. This should incorporate all monthly payments to service providers, as referred to above, as well as the anticipated final account. The use of computer-based spreadsheets or database management systems would improve the efficiency of this process.

11.7   The frequency and detail of the report should be determined by the complexity and value of the particular service contract. For example, expenditure under a mechanical and electrical maintenance contract may be broken down into the following elements:

- planned preventive maintenance
- unplanned/reactive services
- special equipment maintenance.

11.8   On the other hand, a pest control contract might represent a one-line item.

Performance-related Payments

11.9   In order to ensure the continued performance of the service provider against the service specification and SLA, a performance score-sheet should completed regularly by the college so as to arrive at an agreed rating for each service provider. An example format for a performance score-sheet is provided in figure 6.

Figure 6. Performance score-sheet

WESTIN COLLEGE				Month: 9
Item	**Service Criteria**	**Priority Weighting**	**Monthly Rating**	**Score (Weighting x Monthly Rating)**
01	Planned Preventive Maintenance Regime	5	2	10
02	Response Times to Breakdowns	5	0	0
	Total Score			10
	Performance Rating % **(Actual Total/Maximum x 100)**			50 %

Note: In this simple example, the scoring is based upon the following:

    0 = Service does not meet specification
    1 = Service meets specification
    2 = Service exceeds specification

A more detailed scoring system can, however, be employed where a specific measurement system has been agreed.

11.10   The above performance rating can be applied to a performance-related payment table which would reward the service provider for exceeding the specification (if the college has agreed prior to this that they want the performance to be above the previously specified level) and penalise the service provider for not meeting the specification's minimum requirements. The level of detail in the table must be commensurate with the size and complexity of the service provided. However, the golden rule is to concentrate on key performance indicators (KPIs), that is, those that can be determined and analysed cost effectively.

11.11   One aspect of performance which has not been mentioned is the importance of maintaining continuity of service. This is especially so in the case of mechanical and electrical services. Persistent non-functioning of services could have dire consequences for a college. Financial penalties to cover the losses which might be faced by a serious failure have to be carefully considered. However, it is important to set these in the context of the value of contracts. For instance, it would be unreasonable to expect a service provider to accept a level of penalty that was so onerous that any failure would discount all payment.

Change Control

11.12 Colleges must be able to control changes if they are to be in charge of managing their facilities. It is suggested that colleges:

- approve all changes before they are implemented

- before approval, all possible risks are identified together with the impact of the proposed change

- authorisation to proceed with a change should be instructed only by a designated member of the college management or its nominated representative.

11.13 In any event, changes should be avoided unless the consequences are agreed beforehand. Where they are necessary, their cost should be based on tendered prices and rates. Where this is not possible it should be clear that the contract administrator will value the additional works at market rates. The evaluation of changes should always be consistent with the principles of the contract.

Contract Administration

11.14 Contract administration is essential if colleges are to secure continuous improvement in their management of facilities. Successful contract administration includes the following key practices:

- roles and responsibilities should be clearly defined and allocated, with responsibility for the supervision of service delivery vested in the ICF

- every contract (and therefore contractor) should have its own contract manager

- a helpdesk (or central co-ordination point) should be set up to manage the interface between customers and service providers, regardless of whether the service providers are in house or contracted out

- an open-book agreement can be put in place under which the college will have the right to inspect the service provider's accounts for the contract

- frequent meetings should be held with the service provider to discuss performance in the early days of the contract, in order to deal with teething problems. As the contract progresses, the need for such meetings should become less frequent.

Unclear or imprecise roles, responsibilities and targets can inhibit effective teamworking.

Who's in charge?

CASE STUDY

A contracted facilities management company was impeded in its ability to deliver a timely, value-for-money service due to overlapping roles within the college. Although a contract manager had been appointed to act as the college's (client) representative and was the single point of contact, the contractor's facilities manager regularly had to consult a number of in-house managers in the college before a decision could be made. On one occasion, the repair of an item of mechanical plant was delayed because the facilities manager had to approach three managers before finally receiving authorisation for the works to go ahead.

Contract Review

11.15   Contract reviews are necessary in order to establish if the decision to contract out is still valid in terms of the college's facilities management strategy, current market conditions and the performance of the contractor. The necessity of reviews will have been built into the service level agreement (SLA) and formalised in the contract, though here we are concerned primarily with an (internal) college review. The frequency of contract reviews will depend on the size and complexity of the contract, with more frequent reviews likely during the initial period. The following matters must, however, be addressed in each case:

- comparison of tendered and actual costs

- current performance rating

- ideas for improving and/or providing a more cost-effective service

- issues brought quickly to light for discussion, thereby avoiding escalation and further dispute.

Conclusions

11.16   All contracts must be managed, both formal ones with external contractors and informal ones (SLAs) with in-house service providers. The principles and procedures must be appropriate to the contracts being managed and provide a realistic level of flexibility. For these reasons, it is inappropriate to prescribe a single approach; rather, good practice dictates that both the customer-related and financial measures should be considered. It is possible to derive hundreds of performance measures for such services, but it is only key performance indicators that should be captured.

CHECKLIST

This checklist is intended to assist with the review and action planning processes.

		Yes	No	Action needed
a.	Is the college satisfied that its facilities management service contracts properly define the level of payments that should be made and how they should be adjusted when the contractor's performance deviates from that defined as acceptable?	☐	☐	☐
b.	Has the college considered the cashflow implications both for itself and service providers in relation to its management contracts?	☐	☐	☐
c.	Are appropriate cost-monitoring arrangements in place?	☐	☐	☐
d.	Are arrangements in place to enable the continued assessment of the performance of service providers against service specifications and SLAs?	☐	☐	☐
e.	Are adequate controls in place in relation to the agreement of any changes to the services specification and SLAs?	☐	☐	☐
f.	Is the college satisfied with its contract administration and audit arrangements?	☐	☐	☐

Chapter 12

Benchmarking Performance

Introduction

12.1   The purpose of this chapter is to show why benchmarking should be an appropriate tool for facilities management and how it can be applied. Knowing how a college is performing is vital. Without such knowledge, it is difficult to measure the effects of any improvement. For colleges, benchmarking is about establishing the norms for performance in terms of financial, organisational, innovation and change management and customer focus. People tend to have notions of what things might cost, how long they might take and what they should expect. Formalising these notions is essentially what benchmarking is all about.

Policy Considerations

12.2   The following key issues should be taken into consideration.

- benchmarking is an external focus on internal activities and is aimed at supporting the drive towards best practice through continuous improvement. For it to work successfully, benchmarking has to be stakeholder driven, forward-looking, participative and focused on quality and performance

- benchmarking can work well between colleges that would otherwise regard themselves as competitors. Colleges need to recognise that the gains from benchmarking with other colleges far outweigh the perceived disadvantages

- for colleges, the need for benchmarking is perhaps greater than in manufacturing industry. Goods or products can be objectively compared, along with the processes that create them. Facilities management offers no such transparency and relies on policies and procedures which are often ill-defined and poorly documented in comparison

- benchmarking methods are relatively easy to understand and apply. There is a quick and easy way of undertaking benchmarking with respect to facilities management.

Guidance

Continuous Improvement

12.3 Benchmarking is a tool for supporting a process of continuous improvement. Its objective is to identify current performance in relation to best practice in those areas of concern to colleges. It is about measuring performance in the underlying processes of facilities management. This means establishing what colleges are paying for their services and supplies. Typical in these respects are the costs of energy (electricity and gas), other utilities (water, sewerage and telecommunications) and domestic services (cleaning, security and so on).

12.4 Benchmarking can provide college management with a tool to make decisions about policies and procedures in regard to how services should be procured, that is whether they should be contracted out or retained in house. From the findings of visits to colleges, some are already studying the means for deriving benchmarks to help in this decision-making. However, more could and should be done by all colleges: our study has shown that many colleges lacked basic information as regards their estate-related services. Cost or price and performance or quality of service have to become the targets for study if colleges are to be sure of achieving value for money.

Benchmarking Practices

12.5 The main purpose of benchmarking is to measure quality of service and the processes which support them, against the college's goals and aspirations and best-in-class organisations in other sectors. It is 'an external focus on internal activities, functions or operations in order to achieve continuous improvement' (Leibfried and McNair 1994).

12.6 A benchmarking study begins with an analysis of existing activities and practices within the college. These processes have to be properly understood and measurable before comparison can take place with another. Usually, benchmarking is a one-on-one activity; that is, it is used by one organisation to help identify improvements in its own processes by exchanging information in a workshop with another. Normally, the activity is of mutual benefit. An obvious observation is perhaps that it cannot be possible to look so closely at one's competitors. Yet, it is not unknown for colleges to collaborate in benchmarking.

12.7 In partnering arrangements — especially those in which a college is going to share business amongst a few select suppliers — the necessity of benchmarking becomes all the more apparent. Continuous improvement is an integral part of any relationship. By comparing a partner's performance against other service providers, it is possible to provide the stimulus for improvement. This can effectively replace the stimulus for improvement provided by the competitive tendering of each new contract.

Effective Facilities Management — A Good Practice Guide

Measuring Performance

12.8   Benchmarking begins by identifying perceived critical success factors (CSF), typically the strategies, roles and processes existing within the college. Preliminary questions are:

- who is involved in delivering the service?

- why are they involved?

- what are they doing?

- why are they doing it?

- is what they are doing adding value?

12.9   The last of these recognises the need to add value to the services provided to the customer. There are basically eight steps in a benchmarking exercise:

1. identify the subject of the exercise

2. decide what to measure

3. identify who to benchmark both within your sector and outside

4. collect information and data

5. analyse findings and determine gap

6. set goals for improvement

7. implement new order

8. monitor the process for improvement.

Step 1. Identify the subject of the exercise

- agree on the objective(s) of the exercise

- decide on who to involve internally

- define the process (core business or otherwise)

- identify the scope

- set the limits for the exercise

- agree on the process

- produce a flowchart of the process.

Step 2. Decide what to measure

- examine the elements of the process

- establish measures of performance

- verify that measures match objective(s).

Step 3. Identify who to benchmark both within your sector and outside

- identify main competitors and rising stars

- agree those to benchmark

- identify out-of-sector comparisons

- identify best-in-class outside own sector.

Step 4. Collect information and data

- draft a checklist or questionnaire

- pilot the questionnaire

- conduct structured interview(s).

Step 5. Analyse findings and determine gap

- score answers or responses and weight them, as necessary

- analyse qualitative responses

- summarise findings

- measure gap between one's own and others' performance.

Step 6. Set goals for improvement

- identify goals for performance improvement

- establish criteria for judging performance

- draft action plan with agreed milestones for improvement.

Step 7. Implement new order

- draft new procedures

- communicate procedures to all stakeholders

- train those affected by the new order

- implement new process(es).

Step 8. Monitor the process for improvement

- conduct regular review meetings

- observe progress of best-in-class comparison

- determine if any corrective actions are required

- document changes and communicate them to all stakeholders.

Benchmarking in Practice

12.10   Colleges are known to collect data and to engage in their own benchmarking of energy, water, maintenance, cleaning and security costs. Some colleges also participate in benchmarking clubs involving other colleges and in arrangements with very different kinds of organisations. Commercial enterprises have been set up to bring together organisations seeking benchmarking. However, the success of some initiatives is unclear. Colleges should look very closely, therefore, at the costs of getting involved against the likely benefits. The cost of undertaking a benchmarking study of a college's facilities management practices and advising on the findings should be less than £1,000.

Conclusions

12.11   Benchmarking has a place in providing college management with a tool for continuous improvement. Benchmarking provides a simple but effective means for measuring performance and cost, leading to a better understanding of value for money. It can be easily applied and can produce immediate benefits as soon as the results become available.

CHECKLIST

This checklist is intended to assist with the review and action planning processes.

		Yes	No	Action needed
a.	does the college appreciate the importance of benchmarking as a means for measuring its effectiveness in achieving value for money in its facilities management?	☐	☐	☐
b.	has the college made arrangements for the benchmarking of its facilities management performance in terms of the quality of services delivered?	☐	☐	☐
c.	are appropriate arrangements for measuring performance in place?	☐	☐	☐
d.	has the college considered co-operating with other organisations or joining or forming benchmarking clubs to help assess its relative performance in these areas?	☐	☐	☐

Chapter 13

Training and Development

Introduction

13.1   Facilities management could not be described as an established discipline or subject in the UK in the way that architecture and building services might. The subject comes late to the property-related curriculum. However, facilities management has become recognised as a subject in its own right and one that can be studied to postgraduate level in several universities in the UK. The needs and opportunities for education, training and development in facilities management are discussed in this chapter.

Policy Considerations

13.2   The following key issues should be taken into consideration:

- core competence in facilities management covers, amongst other things, property management, financial management, organisational management, innovation and change management, human resources management

- since colleges have to be informed or intelligent clients, the intelligent client function should be a major factor in the drive to have staff who are trained to act as competent college representatives, irrespective of whether or not services are contracted out

- colleges should adopt staff recruitment policies that recognise the specialisation of facilities management and seek individuals who have undergone appropriate education and training and who are prepared to undergo continuous professional development (CPD)

- education and training in facilities management is available in the UK up to the level of master of science. However, little appears to exist at the further education level

- colleges have the opportunity to fill the gap between formal postgraduate study and short duration training courses. This will enable them to educate and train the next generation of the UK's professional facilities managers.

Guidance

Backgrounds of Facilities Managers

13.3   Most facilities managers in colleges are not graduates from schools of facilities management. Rather, they are likely to have a property- or construction-related discipline and career behind them. Architects, civil engineers, building services engineers and accountants have provided the managers of today.

13.4   During the past 10 years colleges and universities have begun to see facilities management as a legitimate subject for study to first degree level and beyond. A few degree courses exist in the UK, but their number could hardly be described as significant. Nevertheless, they provide an important basis for the study of facilities management in a way that is both rigorous and relevant to the needs of business and society at large.

13.5   The results of our survey of colleges revealed that very few facilities managers had formal qualifications in the subject. Many had qualifications falling within the broader property and construction sector. However, most had become converts, so to speak, to the discipline. For them, facilities management might have been seen as an opportunity, a new beginning or, simply, a necessary role to fulfil in a rapidly changing world in which nothing can be guaranteed. The consequence is that many of the people fulfilling the role of facilities manager in colleges do not have the background or experience for the job. That is not to say they are not giving of their best or performing well. Moreover, it does not follow that those whose earlier calling might have been architecture or surveying are better equipped to undertake the work of a facilities manager. Where colleges find expertise lacking they should adopt recruitment policies which recognise the specialisation of facilities management and then seek individuals who have undergone appropriate education and training.

13.6   Excepting personality and preference, successful facilities managers would be those who are able to combine knowledge and skill in property-related matters with an understanding of organisations, people and processes. A good architect does not necessarily make a good facilities manager; understanding how a building works is not the same as ensuring that it is secure and cleaned properly.

13.7   From this simple statement, we should be able to see that facilities management is not just about looking after buildings. As the definition in chapter 1 implies, it is the creation of an environment to support the primary function of the organisation. Knowing how people within an organisation make use of a building — moreover, how those people can perform at their best — is the key to understanding facilities management. For these reasons alone, it is possible to justify the need for clear and distinct education and training in facilities management.

13.8   Colleges need to be informed or intelligent clients (see chapter 1). As such, the ICF should be a major factor in the drive to have staff who are trained to act as competent colleges representatives, irrespective of whether or not services are contracted out.

Core Competence in Facilities Management

13.9 Facilities management draws on a body of knowledge which spans science, engineering, the humanities and social science. Architecture, engineering, construction, technology, management, law and economics are the fields in which the foundations of its core competence are to be found. Facilities managers need to be able to take a physiological view of buildings, rather than a purely anatomical view. This means, in essence, that they have to understand how buildings and other constructed facilities behave and function as environments to support people in their work. A fundamental characteristic of the environment is change and one of the main competencies which facilities managers should have is an ability to manage change.

13.10 Other competencies include organisational management, financial management and customer service. It is the interaction of these which establishes facilities management as a unique discipline. Traditionally, it may have been seen that a good education and training in one of the property-related disciplines was enough. Generally, those educated in one of these specialisations will lack appreciation of the organisational behaviour and human resources management and how innovation and change can be managed effectively. We see core competencies in facilities management covering:

- **property management** building performance, environmental services, workplace design

- **financial management** accounting, finance, purchasing and supply, legal aspects

- **organisational management** organisational structure, behaviour, processes and systems

- **innovation and change management** technology and information management

- **human resources management** motivation, leadership, health and safety.

Studying Facilities Management

13.11 A few UK universities offer facilities management to degree level. University College London and Heriot-Watt University offer postgraduate courses. The Centre for Facilities Management at the University of Strathclyde is perhaps the foremost of UK universities in promoting and providing postgraduate education in facilities management. The centrepiece of their work is the part-time master of science degree in facilities management which runs over two academic years. Contact details appear in annex L.

13.12 Other courses exist in the UK of which many are taken as optional modules or specialisations within broader postgraduate programmes. Whilst the number of degree programmes in the UK might be limited at present, there are many bachelor degree courses in the US and Canada.

13.13 The British Institute of Facilities Management offers a professional qualification for facilities managers. This provides a choice of three main routes:

- direct examination

- higher education

- professional competencies.

13.14 The direct examination and higher education options have an academic focus and involve practical experience. The professional competencies option is, perhaps, more challenging and relies on work and training experience.

13.15 Other examples of training in the private sector which may prove worthwhile are to be found under the following headings:

- facilities operations management (budgeting, purchasing, costing centres, internal charging, critical success factors)

- leading and motivating the facilities management team (human motivation theory and practice, impact of organisational culture)

- optimising space usage and disposing of surplus space

- benchmarking costs and performance

- service level agreements and their management

- managing heating, cooling, comfort and energy costs

- performance-based partnering services contracting.

Continuing Professional Development

13.16 The professional institutions in the UK have, to varying extents, recognised facilities management as an area into which some of their members have moved and for which further opportunities exist. Architects, engineers, surveyors and builders have laid claim to facilities management. Our view is that none of these has a natural claim. Only by refocusing their scope and aims have the institutions managed to appear as though facilities management has a natural place within their jurisdiction.

13.17 In their attempt to promote their members' moves into facilities management, the institutions have encouraged and mounted courses to support continuing professional development (CPD) in the discipline. In this respect, the institutions are fulfilling a valuable role in ensuring that those members who are working in the field or who may wish to do so are receiving up-to-date training of a kind. However these efforts are viewed, they cannot substitute for a comprehensive and rigorous education, training and development programme.

13.18 For facilities managers in colleges, there is the need to be kept up to date in many areas, especially in health and safety matters where legislation is moving quickly. As chapter 8 showed, health and safety legislation is extensive and growing. It is important, therefore, for facilities managers and certain of their colleagues to be kept abreast of current good practice.

Where can Advice be Found?

13.19   There are a number of contact points covering the breadth of facilities management. A useful starting point might be the World Wide Web. Many useful contact names and addresses can be found and not just from an education or training perspective. Examples include:

- British Institute of Facilities Management (BIFM)

- Centre for Facilities Management (CFM), Strathclyde University

- International Facility Managers Association (IFMA)

- Royal Institution of Chartered Surveyors (RICS).

13.20   There are a few periodicals devoted to facilities management, including:

- *Facilities*

- *Facilities Management Journal*

- *Premises and Facilities Management.*

13.21   Other useful information to be found on the World Wide Web includes references, ideas and points of contact covering news, industry matters, cost and benchmarking services, practice guides and forums.

Conclusions

13.22   Facilities management has distinct core competencies which must be present within those managing a college's facilities. Where they are not, retraining or recruitment of appropriate resources will be necessary. Facilities managers can earn recognised qualifications through various centres and institutions. There is a shortage of training opportunities, particularly the availability of courses at the operational level. Irrespective of this shortcoming, facilities managers and those closest to them will need to keep up to date in all areas of their work. For colleges, significant education and training opportunities exist in facilities management.

CHECKLIST

This checklist is intended to assist with the review and action planning processes.

		Yes	No	Action needed
a.	has the college identified core competencies required for the successful implementation of a facilities management strategy and are they available?	☐	☐	☐
b.	does the college bring identified core competencies into its criteria for the recruitment of facilities management staff when required?	☐	☐	☐
c.	are the arrangements for both the college and its service providers for continuing professional development sufficient?	☐	☐	☐

Chapter 14

Private Investment and Partnership

Introduction

14.1   This chapter discusses how the government's requirements for colleges to ensure that opportunities for private investment and partnership can be fully considered and can be made to work effectively for colleges wishing to develop or improve the quality of their facilities. Private sector partnership in developing capital project proposals has already made its mark on the further education sector with the announcement of a number of pathfinder schemes, with more to follow. The aim of this chapter is, therefore, to show the relationship between facilities management and private investment and partnership.

Policy Considerations

14.2   The following key issues should be taken into consideration.

- facilities management is an essential part of any major project proposal and is a key to its likely successful outcome. It may not, however, be appropriate to consider facilities management in relation to smaller schemes

- colleges may be required to market test capital project proposals to fully explore the potential for private sector participation on a value-for-money basis and so need to understand how facilities management can contribute. The requirement to market test schemes will be to an extent commensurate with the nature and scale of the project

- consideration can be given to incorporating facilities management for separate or additional sites within proposed capital schemes. This should be, however, subject to an initial feasibility study to determine potential efficiency gains

- value-for-money considerations must apply at each and every stage. It will be essential to demonstrate that value for money is likely to be achieved, together with the means for measuring it.

- properly defined output specifications are required so that it is clear what is to be provided

- a typical form of private sector participation is that of a design, build, finance and operate (DBFO) scheme which is likely to extend for up to 25 years.

Guidance

Facilities Management and Private Sector Participation

14.3 In any new capital proposal, especially those involving private sector investment or partnership, due consideration must be given at the feasibility stage to the extent of potential facilities management provision. Facilities management will need to be provided on a value-for-money basis and the means for demonstrating this has to be included in any study.

14.4 In all cases, it will be necessary to assess whether or not facilities management is appropriate to the scheme and, if so, in what ways. This can cover those situations in which the bundling of services for other buildings or sites might make the proposed scheme more attractive because of economies of scale. Equally, it may be that facilities management is not suitable for inclusion in the proposed scheme and so should be left out. This may be because the college is already in the throes of market testing its facilities management. Additionally, the college may consider other variations to service provision, such as partial facilities management involving selected services only. Whatever is decided, colleges will need to demonstrate that they have considered the relevance of facilities management to a proposed scheme and the options available for its delivery. A sound articulation of the case for and against, as appropriate, should be provided.

14.5 Colleges will need to consider the mode by which facilities management should be provided. This refers to the choice between in-house service provision and contracting out. The same assessment criteria as apply routinely to assessing capital project proposals for private sector investment and partnership. It is vital to assess risk transfer, including the risks of in-house service provision.

14.6 The Private Finance Panel issued a booklet, *Practical Guidance on the Sharing of Risk and Structuring of PFI Contracts* (Private Finance Panel 1996) and other publications (see annex J) are available to assist at the detailed level of formulating and progressing a such proposals. In the case of risk, the Private Finance Panel drew attention to risks affecting projects:

- design and construction (to time and cost)
- commission and operation (including maintenance)
- demand, volume and usage
- residual value
- technology and obsolescence
- regulation and similar risks, such as taxation and planning permission
- project finance.

Output Specification

14.7   Earlier chapters, notably chapters 7 and 11, have proposed procedures for specifying service requirements. It is essential to advance consideration of facilities management in any capital project proposal likely to include private sector investors or developers to the point where all of the issues and likely actions have been considered. The thoroughness that should apply to specifying service requirements without direct private sector participation should apply to the same extent to those schemes with it. Colleges may find this easier to achieve in some cases, since they may be unencumbered by past arrangements when contemplating an entirely new scheme.

Criteria for Success

14.8   The crucial criteria for assessing direct private sector involvement in capital project proposals are value for money and risk transfer. However, a balance has to be struck between the two so that colleges should not be seeking the maximum risk transfer, but the most appropriate. The latter is likely to secure best value for money. Most appropriate risk transfer occurs when responsibility for risks is allocated to those who are best placed to manage them.

Conclusions

14.9   Private sector participation in one form or another is likely to be increasingly important for the financing, provision and management of colleges' capital project proposals. Facilities management is a key element in all design, build, finance and operate (DBFO) proposals. Colleges are free to consider many options, but whatever they do they must demonstrate rigour. This is arguable no more so than in the areas of risk transfer and value for money. It will also be important to ensure that appropriate priority is assigned between capital procurement, financing and facilities management aspects of project proposals.

CHECKLIST

This checklist is intended to assist with the review and action planning processes.

		Yes	No	Action needed
a.	is the college aware of the importance of facilities management provision being considered in relation to the market testing of capital project proposals of the government's private finance initiative?	☐	☐	☐
b.	is the college aware of the private finance panel's advice on the risk affecting partnership projects?	☐	☐	☐
c.	are the college's property facilities management requirements properly reflected in the output specifications for partnership schemes?	☐	☐	☐
d.	is the college aware of the balance between value for money and risk transfer in assessing partnership proposals and the facilities management elements contained therein?	☐	☐	☐

Annexes

Role of the Informed Client Function

- understand the organisation, its culture, its customers and needs
- understand and clearly specify service requirements and targets
- manage the implementation of contracting out
- risk management — minimise risk to the organisation's continuation
- agree monitoring standards
- manage contractors and monitor their performance
- benchmark performance of contracted-out service(s)
- survey users for satisfaction with the service
- provide relevant management reports to users
- review service levels and requirements to ensure they still meet user needs
- develop with the contractor service delivery strategies
- agree changes to service requirements with the contractor
- maintain the capability to re-tender
- understand the facilities management market and how it is developing
- strategic planning
- safeguard public funds
- develop its own skills through training.

Relationships with Suppliers

adapted from HM Government, *Setting New Standards: A Strategy for Government Procurement* (HMSO 1995)

Getting the Relationship Right

The best contribution that colleges can make to the enhancement of the competitiveness of suppliers is to manage their own procurement intelligently and well. An important element of this will be to combine competition and co-operation to optimal effect.

Mutually satisfactory relationships between buyers and sellers are fundamental to successful procurement activity. There is a wide range of possible relationships. At one end, both sides will be mainly concerned to optimise their immediate interests without making long-term commitments. Such relationships are typical of many commodity markets. At the other end of the range, both sides will look for a long-term, co-operative partnership. What type of relationship will produce the greatest benefits will depend upon circumstances such as the nature of the market and the requirement. Choosing the right relationship with suppliers and managing it well requires skill, judgement and experience.

Whatever the chosen relationship with suppliers, colleges will avoid taking an unnecessarily adversarial or unhelpful approach. Relationships will be as open and supportive as possible, given the need to maintain competition and to treat suppliers even-handedly and will be based on mutual respect. Colleges will recognise that it is in their interests to help suppliers develop in ways which make them better able to provide what the college requires to the desired quality and at a competitive price. The relationship will be one which encourages continuous improvement.

Partnering

There is a great deal of current interest in partnering or partnership sourcing as the basis of relationships with suppliers. The term refers to arrangements under which customers and suppliers decide to collaborate closely in order to deliver requirements such as cost reduction, improved quality or innovative solutions, rather than to conduct all their business at arm's length. Although co-operation will normally be more beneficial than an adversarial relationship, there are important conditions for partnering which must apply, particularly, in the public sector:

- there must be competition at the outset to select the partner and periodic re-competition thereafter

- there must be a clear definition of the contractual responsibilities of both parties

- there should be specific and measurable milestones for improved performance as part of the contract with a partner.

Annex B

Partnering is likely to bring greater benefits than alternative approaches in certain circumstances, for example where there is a poorly developed or highly specialised market or where the requirements of the purchaser are complex and continuously developing. Purchasing officers should consider carefully whether or not a partnering arrangement would best suit the needs of their college in particular cases.

Strategy Implementation

- the informed or intelligent client should be given the responsibility for implementing the decision to contract out

- there should be senior management commitment to the successful implementation of this

- they should perform a risk assessment to identify risks arising from the implementation of contracting out, particularly the impact on core operations, and how to address these. They should then assign responsibilities for dealing with these. Typical risks include:

  — unclear definition of roles and responsibilities

  — a timetable that is too demanding

  — insufficient time allowed for contract negotiation

  — insufficient expertise in the negotiation of contracts and drafting of SLAs

  — lack of definition of requirements before contract award

  — the transition period between the award and start of contract

- they should also consider the effect of a major breakdown in the contracted-out service and make contingency plans

- colleges should plan the arrangements for managing the transition period. For example, they should plan the handover of information to the new contractor. They should allow sufficient time for this (two to three months) and ensure that the information is correct

- in the transition period before the contract starts, the new contractor should visit user staff and tell them what is now expected of them (for example, new procedures, new attitudes).

Prevention of Fraud and Irregularity in the Award and Management of Contracts

adapted from HM Treasury, *Estates and Building Services Procurement: Prevention of Fraud and Irregularity in the Award and Management of Contracts*, (TSO 1996)

Definitions

Fraud may be defined as the use of deception with the intention of obtaining an advantage. Corruption is the giving or receiving of money, goods or services for favours provided. The risks of fraud and corruption can be reduced by awareness of their nature and good procurement practice. Fraud should be deterred. Similarly, prevention is always preferable to detection. Strong preventive controls should therefore be applied.

Risks

Property maintenance services have long been considered to carry a high risk of fraud, corruption and other irregularity. The frauds can take a number of forms, some involving collusion with the college's personnel or agents.

One fraud risk is the 'ringing' of contracts, whereby a group of contractors conspire to form a ring for submitting tenders ostensibly in competition but, in fact, having arranged amongst themselves which firm will bid the lowest. Even the lowest tender will be overpriced. The aim of the ring will be to win the majority of the contracts available and share them.

Frauds can be perpetrated in the execution or pricing of work for new maintenance contracts. This can take a variety of forms from failure to perform to specification, to deliberate falsification of suppliers' invoices or labour records leading to overpayment for services. Grounds maintenance contracts also provide opportunities for a contractor to claim for more work than has been done, with or without collusion.

The pricing of contracts not let by competitive tender carries the risk that costs may be deliberately overstated. This can be a particular problem in 'cost plus' contracts and in small value non-competitive contracts which can add up to large amounts of expenditure over the year.

Particular care needs to be taken about the acceptance of gifts, hospitality and other benefits, and to ensure there is no conflict of interest in the award of contracts.

Key Principles of Control

There are a number of basic principles of control to minimise the risk of fraud in estates-related services and facilities management procurement.

Separation of Duties

Duties should be separated to ensure that no single member of staff has control over the award and procurement process for contracts. For example, there should be a separation of duties between ordering the work, certification and authorisation of payments. Failure to separate duties is one of the most common elements of fraud in this context.

Colleges should also ensure that all staff are aware of the risks of fraud and of their responsibilities for reporting any fraud or suspicions of fraud to the appropriate level of management. One option is to set up an internal fraud helpline.

Authorisation

All transactions or specified activities should be approved or sanctioned by a manager or other responsible person before they are undertaken. Limits for these authorisations should be specified. Authorisation seeks to ensure that proper responsibility is taken for all transactions and activities. Authorisation should ensure that delegated limits are complied with, provide independent scrutiny and consistency in the procurement process.

Competitive Tendering

Contracts should normally be let by competition. A decision not to use competitive tendering should require a higher level of authority.

Regular Supervision

There should be positive supervision of the procurement process including regular and unannounced checks of transactions. In addition, managers should carry out pre-commitment checks to confirm the need for the service; that the type of contract is appropriate; and that estimated costs are realistic.

Record-keeping

Appropriate records must be kept to enable every decision and transaction to be traced through the system. The requirement to keep proper records is an important deterrent to fraud.

Documentation

Standard documentation, in the sense of being uniform and consistent, can help to enforce conformity with procedures and legal requirements.

Budgetary Control

Budgetary control matches resources and costs to responsibilities for objectives and outputs. Managers should be fully accountable for the achievement of their objectives and targets. Budgets should be closely linked to planning and review procedures to ensure that proposed expenditure is essential. This will help to minimise the risk of fraud.

Indicators of Fraud

The following may indicate the occurrence of fraud in the tendering and award of contracts for estate-related services and facilities management:

- contracts that do not make commercial sense

- contracts that include special, but unnecessary, specifications that only a favoured supplier could meet

- consistent use of single source contracts

- split ordering to circumvent contract conditions

- contractors who are qualified and capable of tendering, but who do not do so for no apparent reason

- unusual patterns of consistently high accuracy in estimating tender costs — this is used to deflect the attention of auditors and senior managers who tend to look for adverse rather than favourable variances

- withdrawal of the lowest tenderer without obvious reason and who may then go on to become a subcontractor of a high tenderer

- there appear to be patterns in tenders from a group of firms, for example, fixed rotation of the lowest tender

- a certain contractor may tender substantially higher on some tenders for no logical cost justification

- tender prices appear to drop whenever a new tenderer submits a bid

- obvious links between contractors tendering for these works (for example, companies sharing the same address, having the same directors, managers and professional advisers)

- acceptance of late bids

- disqualification of suitable tenderer

- change in tender after other bids are opened, often by the drafting of deliberate mistakes into initial tender

- poor documentation of the contract awarding process

- suppliers who are awarded contracts disproportionate to their size

- contracts awarded to contractors with poor performance record

- unexplained changes in contract shortly after award

- the successful tenderer repeatedly subcontracts work to companies that submitted higher tenders

- a consistent pattern appears of the same winners and losers (from the tender lists)

- undue patronage, by consistently favouring one firm or a small number of firms over others

- close personal relationships between staff and suppliers.

Declarations of Interests

Colleges shall require staff and management to declare any personal interests in proposed contracts and put in place appropriate administrative arrangements to facilitate this. 'Relevant interests' for this purpose could include not only financial interests but also interests such as membership of other public bodies or closed organisations. The duty to decline would also extend to the interests of persons closely connected with the manager or staff member, such as his or her spouse/partner and the close family of the individual or of the spouse/partner.

Risks and Controls

Colleges should consider at invitation to tender acknowledgement stage or at bid submission a formal request to the tenderer to sign to the effect that no fraud or corrupt practice has occurred when developing the bid. This has two effects:

- **deterrent** the contractor is alerted to the fact that the client is aware of the risk of fraud and will be on the look-out for any evidence that it has occurred

- **protective** it ensures that should something fraudulent come to light, there can be no excuse that the company was not aware of college policy.

Colleges will need to handle such a declaration with sensitivity so as not to impair good working relationships with suppliers or service providers. Tables 1 and 2 show the risks of which colleges should be aware, and suggested control factors that can be used to minimise the risk.

Table 1. Risks and controls in the award of contracts

Activity	Risk	Control
Scoping of contract	The contract specification is written in a manner which favours a particular supplier.	Use of contract panel consisting of technical, end-user and buying representatives, to ensure that more than one person is involved in drawing up the specification.
Contract documentation	Conditions of contract are changed to accommodate a favoured supplier and/or exclude competitors who cannot meet the varied conditions.	Standard contract conditions and specification to be used. Any variations to be approved by senior management.
Setting evaluation criteria	Original evaluation criteria are changed after the receipt of submissions to ensure that favoured suppliers are shortlisted.	Use evaluation criteria as agreed by the contract panel prior to tendering. Where EU procurement directives apply, evaluation criteria are required to be stated in advance.
Selection of tenderers	The selection of a group of tenderers with a view to ensuring that the favoured tenderer will win.	Selection by panel against clearly defined and objective criteria; where applicable, in accordance with the requirements of EU procurement directives.
Tendering	Contract rings — repeat orders using narrow source list. Links between contractors — uncompetitive.	Firms should be selected by someone other than the member of staff commissioning the work. Widen the sourcing list by the introduction of new firms and examine tender records for a pattern of pricing and tenderers who have been awarded contracts. Check for links in names, addresses and numbers plus tendering partners.
telephone		
Tender evaluation	Collusion to ensure that the favoured supplier is chosen.	Technical and commercial evaluation to be carried out independently by the contract panel.
Post-tender negotiations	Modification of favoured supplier's tender to ensure they are successful.	Where necessary, identify reasons for negotiation and negotiate with a minimum of two suppliers.
Single source procurement	Overstating of prices.	Competitive tendering and advance purchase planning. Tight budgetary control and a comprehensive system of price checking.

Table 2. Risks and controls in the management of contracts

Activity	Risk	Control
Contractual correspondence	Altering terms and conditions to suit favoured supplier.	Contract terms and conditions will be the procurement team's and may not be altered without senior management approval.
Contract management	False claims for work not carried out or exaggerated claims for actual work done.	Clear audit trail with written records. Authorisation of changes, by senior management, to original document. Site checks, random and systematic.
Claims negotiation	Assisting the contractor to justify claims.	Claims negotiation should be carried out using professional advisers.
Certification of completion	Inadequate certification may lead to overpayments or payment for work not carried out.	Clear separation of duties between ordering the work, certification and authorisation for payment. Ensure that certified documents are not returned to the originator.
Authorisation	Contract splitting to keep contract values under particular staff member's authorised financial limit.	The splitting of contracts should not be allowed unless authorised by senior management. Manager's and supervisors' checks and sampling should be constructed to detect this.
Acceptance of documentation to support claims	Documentation has been modified or fabricated.	Act on original documents. Do not accept copies or faxes. Do not accept use of correction fluids and so on without obtaining satisfactory explanations for any amendments.
Supervision	Payment for work not done and duplication. Failure to monitor daywork on site. Duplication of names on more than one return or 'ghost' workers. Work paid for under one contract and provided in a different format on another contract. Lack of separation of duties, failure to report gifts and hospitality or conflicts of interest.	Good site supervision and audit of site diary. Look for similar work in same building and enforce contract management controls. Separate duties, ensure hospitality rules are formulated and understood, have clear conduct and discipline code including conflicts of interests and penalties, take disciplinary action against those staff who fail to declare a conflict of interest.
Security of documents	Duplication and manipulation of accountable documents.	Restricted access to accountable documents such as works and stores orders, tender documents and claim forms. Serial numbering should be used.

Risks Involved in Contracting Out

adapted from NAO and Information Technology Services Agency, *Outsourcing Service Delivery Operations* (HMSO 1996)

Planning to Contract Out

- are the objectives for contracting out correctly identified?

- is the service to be contracted out adequately scoped and defined?

- are the in-house costs of delivering the business to be contracted out adequately calculated?

- will adequate competition be generated from credible contractors?

- does the contracted-out management team have the right numbers and mix of skills?

Shortlisting Potential Contractors

- are there appropriate evaluation criteria?

- are there adequate safeguards against corruption or bias in the evaluation?

- is there sufficient expertise on the evaluation team?

Negotiating Contracts

- are customer needs translated into business requirements?

- are measures of contractor performance defined?

- are appropriate penalties for unsatisfactory contractor performance included in the contracts?

- is the college contract protected against the contractors making excessive profits?

- are there contingency arrangements that would apply in the event of disasters defined?

- are there adequate safeguards against the commercial failure of the contractor?

- are termination arrangements specified?

- are there adequate safeguards to protect the confidentiality of data?

- are there appropriate arrangements for the control of assets?

- are there plans for transferring staff in an orderly fashion?

- is adequate audit access provided for in the contracts?

Tender Assessment

- have the evaluation criteria been tested thoroughly?

- have the contractors' price proposals and their experience in delivering equivalent business been tested thoroughly?

- are there safeguards against corruption or bias in the selection of contractors?

- is there sufficient expertise in the evaluation teams?

- are there safeguards against the possibility of legal challenge by contractors?

Contract Award

- are there adequate skills in the negotiating team?

- is the significance of contract terms properly assessed?

- are there safeguards against disruption to existing business prior to the handover of business to the successful contractors?

Contract Management

- are there adequate arrangements to manage the contracts after award, including performance monitoring and price control mechanism?

Contractual Approach and Terms

- the contract should normally be for a period of three to five years. Colleges may wish to include a provision for the option of extending this by a further one to two years

- colleges should ensure that contract documentation is consistent with the specification

- colleges should consider using the Chartered Institute of Purchasing and Supply model facilities management agreement and should ensure that their contract provisions are in line with Central Unit on Procurement (CUP) *Guidance Note 42* (see annex M for details)

- the contract should include provisions for:

  — colleges to retain ownership of, and access to, all relevant records and knowledge

  — the arrangements for another contractor to take over the service at short notice in the event of contractor financial failure

  — the handling of changes in the college's requirements

  — full disclosure of all data via an open-book arrangement which gives the college access to all the contractor's premises, systems, books and records

  — the college's right to check the qualifications and competencies of the personnel the contractor proposes to use and to approve any appointment beforehand

  — requiring the contractor and any subcontractors to have in place quality assurance or quality management systems

  — contingency arrangements

  — the arrangements for the transfer of assets at the start and end of the contract

  — the mechanisms for dispute resolution

  — the arrangements for handover to a succeeding contractor at the end of the contract

- if the contract involves a one-off transfer of assets to the successful bidder, it should include a clawback provision to allow the college to share the benefit if the contractor then sells them on. The contract should contain clear and precise terms which:

  — detail service levels and performance standards the contractor is required to meet

- — define performance monitoring arrangements and the associated information requirements

- — link payment to performance

- — detail any remedies in the event of default of whatever nature

- colleges may wish to guarantee the expected workload for the first few years of a contract, in order to generate enough interest from potential bidders. If *TUPE* applies, the contract should stipulate that, at the end of the contract, the existing contractor will have to provide other bidders with information about the staff who would transfer to them under this

- the contract should set out the pricing regime:

  - — fixed price for items or tasks which can be defined fully

  - — variable price for those which cannot

  - — arrangements for sharing savings

- the payment structure should provide the contractor with an incentive to perform well, for example by:

  - — paying nothing until the required performance standards are met

  - — making subsequent payments dependent on continuing to meet these standards

  - — structuring payments to provide incentives to improve performance

  - — making good identified failures at the contractor's cost

  - — recovery of costs incurred by colleges in rectifying the poor performance

  - — the removal of particular services from the contractor

  - — in exceptional circumstances, the right to terminate the contract

- colleges should require appropriate third-party protection in the form of parent or associated company guarantees, performance bonds, and evidence of the appropriate insurance cover

- the contract should normally reserve the college's right to terminate the contract in the event of a change in the controlling interest in the contractor

- the contract should ensure that the contractor cannot assign any part of the contract to a third party without the college's agreement

- contracts should be consistent internally and with each other

- the contract should be flexible enough to cope with any client-approved changes in user requirements over the course of the contract.

General Conditions of Contract for the Provision of Services

taken from CUP *Guidance Note 42, Contracting for the Provision of Services*

1. Definitions

2. Services

3. Recovery of sums due

4. Value-added tax

5. Bankruptcy

6. Racial discrimination

7. Transfer, sub-letting and subcontracting

8. Corrupt gifts and payments of commission

9. Drawings, specifications and other data

10. Use of documents, information etc.

11. Disclosure of information

12. Law

13. Arbitration

14. *Official Secrets Act*

15. Security measures

16. Approval for admission to government premises and information about work people

17. Observance of regulations

18. Safety

19. Accidents to contractors' servants or agents

20. Special health and safety hazards

21. Liability in respect of damage to government property

22. Contractor's property

23. Intellectual property rights

24. Patents

25. Default

26. Insurance

27. Duty of care

28. Design liability

29. Issues of government property

30. Personal injury and loss of property

Annex F

31. Hours of work

32. Occupation of government premises

33. Contractor's organisation

34. Break

35. Facilities provided

36. Duration of contracts

37. Variation of requirement

38. Contract documents

39. Amendments to contracts

40. Monitoring and liaison meetings

41. Price

42. Price fixing

43. Lead-in costs

44. Payment

45. Payment of subcontractors

46. Availability of information

47. National Audit Office access

48. Transfer of responsibility

49. Quality assurance

Sections for a Service Level Agreement

taken from CUP *Guidance Note 44* (see annex M for details)

1. Definitions

2. Services

3. Value-added tax

4. Subcontracting

5. Resolution of dispute

6. Default

7. Duty of care

8. Hours of work

9. Occupation of premises

10. Agreement holder's organisation

11. Break

12. Facilities provided

13. Terms of agreement

14. Variation of requirement

15. Agreement documentation

16. Amendments to agreement

17. Monitoring and liaison meetings

18. Price

19. Extensions

20. Allocation of costs

21. Transfer of responsibility

Example of a Service Specification

Cleaning Contract for Libraries, Reading Rooms, Quiet Rooms, and Theatres

Daily tasks

1. Empty rubbish containers and bins (clean as required). Collect all rubbish and waste material, place in receptacle provided by the contractor and remove to the nearest agreed disposal point.

2. Sweep floors using appropriate anti-static mop sweeper, leaving floors clean and free from visible dirt, dust and smears.

3. Lift primary matting and vacuum beneath.

4. Vacuum all soft floors and carpeted areas (loose or fitted). This is to include all raised platforms, stages, stairways etc.

5. Spot clean hard floors

6. Spot clean tables, desks and chairs.

Weekly tasks

1. Damp wipe furniture, fittings and horizontal surfaces.

2. Using high-speed vacuum floor polishing machines, spray clean hard floor areas with an approved cleaning agent and maintainer and appropriate brush or pads until floor is cleaned and polished.

Performance requirements

1. Ensure that bins and other containers for waste and rubbish are emptied regularly so that they are not allowed to remain full.

2. Do not permit the contents of bins and other containers to pose a threat to health or allow them to detract from the normal enjoyment of the rooms by their users.

3. Ensure that all floors are maintained in a clean, enduring and non-slip state, free from debris and other deleterious materials.

4. Do not permit spillage, contaminants or other deleterious materials to remain on floors.

5. Ensure that all work surfaces, fittings and other furnishings remain free from accumulated dust and other debris and that they are maintained in a condition that does not detract from the normal enjoyment of the rooms by their users.

6. Do not permit spillage, contaminants or other deleterious materials to remain on work surfaces, fittings and other furnishings.

Example of a Service Level Agreement

adapted from information provided by IBM and Johnson Controls

Performance Reports

Service performance reports will be completed each month on the last working day by the service provider. Whilst it will be the service provider's duty to complete the reports, the employer will provide the service provider with a master service performance record sheet. These records will record the following items:

- maintenance details — incidence of maintenance-induced failures, adherence to agreed PPM schedules

- job card — responses and actions within service level

- security — compliance with security procedures, absence of misuses or losses

- cleaning — completion of all specified items

- safety — completion of all minuted action items

- space and facilities planning — space database kept up to date, users informed of progress

- reception — procedure for dealing with visitors is followed

- reprographics — photocopiers serviced within four hours

- stationery and printing — orders fulfilled on a timely basis

- fax service — availability of service maintained.

Operations and Service Assessment

Operations and service assessment will be undertaken adopting the same procedure as for service performance records. This assessment will record the following items:

- effective communication — timely reporting, prompt response to requests

- documentation — complete, sufficient, on time, maintained

- additional work — positive attitude, flexibility, proactiveness

- image — general housekeeping, staff appearance

- management and co-ordination — efficient use of resources, protect client interests

- process and methods of work — innovative proposals and effective solutions

Annex I

- supplier relationships — control of supplier performance, quality of supplier performance

- feedback — space utilisation opportunities, advice on locations

- financial — fully evaluated proposals, well-structured business cases.

Performance Measures

The following performance measures will apply to monthly service performance records:

- criteria met or exceeded — yes (score 1); no (score 0) for each item

- total service performance must score no less than 8 at each monthly assessment.

The following performance measures will apply to operations and services assessment:

- criteria exceeded, met or failed — exceed (score 2); meet (score 1); fail (score 0) for each item

- total service performance must score no less than 9 at each monthly assessment.

The above performance measures will be used to determine overall contract performance for the service provider.

Guidance on the Private Finance Initiative

issued by the Private Finance Panel

HM Treasury, *Private Opportunity, Public Benefit: Progressing the private finance initiative* (November 1995)

HM Treasury, *Guidelines for Smoothing the Procurement Process* (April 1996)

HM Treasury, *Risk and Reward in PFI Contracts* (May 1996)

HM Treasury, *5 Steps to the Appointment of Advisers to PFI Projects* (May 1996)

HM Treasury, *Writing an Output Specification* (October 1996)

HM Treasury, *Transferability of Equity* (October 1996)

HM Treasury, *Basic Contractual Terms* (October 1996)

HM Treasury, *PFI in Government Accommodation* (October 1996)

Useful Names and Addresses

British Institute of Facilities
Management (BIFM)
67 High Street
Saffron Walden
Essex CB10 1AA

Tel: 01799 508608
Fax: 01799 513237
email: admin@bifm.org.uk

Building Cost Information Service of
RICS (BCIS)
75–87 Clarence Street
Kingston-upon-Thames KT1 1RB

Tel: 0181 546 7554
Fax: 0181 547 1238
email: 100435.2525@compuserve.co.uk

Business Round Table, The
18 Devonshire Street
London W1N 1FS

Tel: 0171 636 6951
Fax: 0171 636 6952
email: brp-groome@dial.pipex.com

The Public Enquiries Unit
HM Treasury
Room 110/2
Parliament Street
London SW1P 3AG

Tel: 0171 270 4558
Fax: 0171 270 5244
email: info@hm-treasury.gov.uk

Centre for Facilities Management
Strathclyde Graduate Business School
199 Cathedral Street
Glasgow G4 0QU

Tel: 0141 553 4165/6000
Fax: 0141 552 7299

Chartered Institute of Building (CIOB)
Englemere
Kings Ride
Ascot
Berkshire SL5 7TB

Tel: 01344 630700
Fax: 01344 630777
www.ciob.org.uk/

Health and Safety Executive (HSE)
Rose Court
2 Southwark Bridge
London SE1 9HS

Tel: 0171 717 6000
Fax: 0171 717 6717

Heriot-Watt University
Riccarton
Edinburgh EH14 4AS

Tel: 0131 451 3090
Fax: 0131 451 3002

Annex K

The Joint Contracts Tribunal for the
Standard Form of Building Contract (JCT)
82 New Cavendish Street
London W1M 8AD

Tel: 0171 580 5588
Fax: 0171 323 1590

Private Finance Panel
3rd Floor
61–71 Victoria Street
London SW1H 0XA

Tel: 0171 468 6500
Fax: 0171 222 3470
email: @pfpe.demon.co.uk

Royal Institution of Chartered Surveyors
(RICS)
12 Great George Street
Parliament Square
London SW1P 3AD

Tel: 0171 222 7000
Fax: 0171 222 9430

University College London
Gower Street
London WC1E 6BT

Tel: 0171 387 7050
Fax: 0171 387 8057

Abbreviations

BPR	Business process re-engineering
CDM	*Construction, Design and Management Regulations 1994*
COSHH	*Control of Substances Hazardous to Health Regulations 1988*
CPD	continuous professional development
CSF	critical success factor
CUP	Central Unit on Procurement
DBFO	design, build, finance and operate
EC	European Community
HRM	human resources management
HSE	Health and Safety Executive
IiP	Investors in People
ICF	informed (or intelligent) client function
IT	information technology
JCT	Joint Contracts Tribunal
KPI	key performance indicator
NEBOSH	National Examinations Board in Occupational Safety and Health
OJEC	*Official Journal of the European Communities*
PPM	planned preventive maintenance
PPE	personal protective equipment
QA	quality assurance
RIDDOR	*Reporting of Injuries, Diseases and Dangerous Occurrences Regulations 1995*
SLA	service level agreement
SWOT	strengths, weaknesses, opportunities and threats
TUPE	*Transfer of Undertakings (Protection of Employment) Regulations 1981*
VFM	value for money

Bibliography

Barrett, P. S. (Ed.) (1995) *Facilities Management: Towards best practice*, Oxford, Blackwell Science

Business Round Table, The (1996) *Thinking about Facilities Management*, London, The Business Round Table Ltd

CUP (1991) Note 30, *Specification Writing*, HM Treasury

——(1993) Note 42, *Contracting for the Provision of Services*, HM Treasury

——(1994) Note 44, *Service Level Agreements*, HM Treasury

——(1996) Note 54, *Value Management*, HM Treasury

FEFC, Chesterton International plc and NAO (1996) *Estate Management in Further Education Colleges: A Good Practice Guide*, London, HMSO

FEFC and NAO (1997) *Procurement: A Good Practice Guide*, London, The Stationery Office

Gadde, Lars-Erik (1996) *Supplier Management in the Construction Industry: Working papers*, Gothenburg, Chalmers University of Technology

HSE (1995) *Everyone's Guide to RIDDOR: Reporting of Injuries, Diseases and Dangerous Occurrences Regulations 1995*, Sudbury, HSE Books

HM Government (1995) *Setting New Standards: A strategy for government procurement*, (Cm 2840), London, HMSO

HM Treasury (1996) *Estates and Building Services Procurement: Prevention of fraud and irregularity in the award and management of contracts* (DAO/GEN 17/96), London, The Stationery Office

Leibfried, Kathleen H. J. and C J McNair. (1994) *Benchmarking: A tool for continuous improvement*, New Jersey, John Wiley

Information Technology Services Agency (1996) *Outsourcing the Service Delivery Operations,* London, HMSO

Private Finance Panel (1996) *Practical Guidance on the Sharing of Risk and Structuring of Private Finance Initiative Contracts*, London, Private Finance Panel

Index

accommodation strategy 2.6

accounting 9.15; 9.17

appraisal *see* performance

audit 2.8–2.10; 3.22

benchmarking 12.2; 12.3–12.4; clubs 12.10, identifying 12.8

CDM *see* legislation

change management 11.12

charters 6.12

communication 2.21

contracting out *see* outsourcing; *see also* contracts

contractors 9.13–9.16; *see also* outsourcing

contracts 3.23–3.24; 5.15–5.17; 5.20; 5.21–5.23; 7.2; 7.32; 9.16; annex F, terms of 11.2–11.3, administration of 11.14–11.15

core business 1.3–1.4; 2.3; 2.11

CPD *see* staff development

critical success factor 7.17–7.20

CSF *see* critical success factor

customers 3.4; 5.9–10; 6.10; 7.26

disability 8.11

EC *see* European Community

education *see* staff development

employment law 4.6–4.8; 5.11–5.14

European Community, directives of 5.15–5.16; 5.26

facilities management, definition of 1.2; 1.6–1.8; 13.2–13.10, strategies for 2.2–2.5; 2.18; annex C, study of 13.1–13.2; 13.3–13.5; 13.11–13.15; 13.19–13.21, total 9.2; 9.17–9.20

finance 11.4; 11.6

fraud annex D

health and safety 7.7; 8.2; 8.4–8.5; 8.9; 8.12

helpdesks 10.12

ICF *see* informed client function

in-house 3.2; 3.13–3.22; 4.4–4.5; 4.9–4.10; 5.8; 5.35; 6.2–6.3; 6.8; 6.11–6.14

informed client function 1.12; 2.25; 3.13; 11.2; annex A

intelligent client function *see* informed client function

IT *see* technology

KPI *see* performance

legislation 8.3; 8.4–8.5

managing agent 9.7–9.12

market testing 3.22; 9.3; 14.4

non-core business 1.3–1.4; 2.3; 2.11

outsourcing 3.2; 3.13–3.23; 3.25; 4.4–4.5; 5.3; 5.8; 5.12; 6.4; annex E; annex F

partnering 1.17, 3.17; 10.7–10.9; 12.7; annex B

performance, measures of 4.13; 7.2; 7.17–7.20; 7.21–7.23; 12.8, pay related 11.9–11.10

PFI *see* private investment partnership

private investment partnership 14.2; 14.6; annex J

procurement 2.23; 3.16; 5.4–5.6;

productivity 7.18

purchasing *see* procurement

QA *see* quality

quality 5.29–5.31; 7.27; 7.30–7.32

resources, use of 2.22

risk 1.9; 3.7–3.10; 9.20; annex E

service provision 9.6–9.20; 10.2–10.4; annex B

service specification 7.2; 7,5; 7.7–7.11; 7.28–7.29; 14.7; annex H

service level agreements 3.13; 5.18–5.19; 6.12; 7.2; 7.5–7.6; 7.12–7.16; 7.28–7.29; 11.2; annex G; annex I

SLA *see* service level agreements

space utilisation 2.8

staff development 2.20; 4.11–4.12; 6.8–6.9; 13.16–13.18

stakeholders 2.21; 5.9–10; 6.6–6.7; 7.2–7.4

strategic plan 2.3; 2.6

subcontracting 9.17

supplier *see* service provision

technology 3.17; 6.14

tendering 5.15–5.16; 5.18–5.19; 5,24–5.28; 5.31